inside:

ARCHITECTURE AND DESIGN

A guide to the practice of architecture

(what they don't teach you in architecture school)

Table of Contents

Preface 9

Introduction...11

Getting Your First Job 15

    When to start working 15

    Finding the right firm.................................17

    Resume Tips...21

    The Cover Letter...24

    The Resume 25

    The Portfolio 30

    The Interview..31

    Negotiations 39

    Your first day 40

Architecture as a Business 43

    Budgets 44

    Schedules 46

    Client Input..48

    Contracts 51

    Consultants..51

    Contractors..54

    Finding work..55

    Politics 57

    Home Owners Associations 58

    School Board of Directors 59

    Planning and Zoning Commission 60

    City Council 61

    Business Management................................63

Identifying Potential Projects............................69

Custom Residential Design 70

Other Residential Projects 70

Mutli-family...71

Commercial Retail..71

Municipal..72

Education 72

Healthcare 73

Office Buildings/Tenant Improvements 73

Other Commercial 73

Getting the job..74

Finding work by Word of Mouth..75

Finding the client...78

Request for Qualifications 80

Finding work by Internet 85

Initial Project Analysis 91

Programming...92

Define Project Scope..99

Getting the team together 103

Consultants...106

Site Analysis/Existing Conditions 108

Field Measures 111

The importance of initial project analysis 115

Initial Designs 119

Schematic Design..119

Design Development 129

Construction types:..135

Construction Documents 143

The Drawings..143

Organizing your drawing set...150

Specifications 157

Bidding and Negotiation 163

Design-Bid-Build 165

The reality of Design-Bid-Build 172

Construction Manager 175

The reality of Construction Manager 179

Design Build 180

Reality of Design-Build 185

Be a professional 186

Construction Administration 189

Architects role in CA 189

Meetings 191

Documentation 197

Payments 200

Design Opportunities 203

Project Closeout 206

Interns in CA 208

Conclusion 213

Appendix A: Common Abbreviations 217

Preface

inside: Architecture and Design was created to give future architects, interns and licensed architects the information they need to succeed in the field of architecture. It intended to be a reference book and guide to what really happens in architecture, everything they don't teach you in school.

The book goes through a progression, starting with getting your first job, then to understanding the firm, getting a project and finally following through with the design. The intention is to walk you through every step you will take in your career and throughout the project. There are a lot of tips and tricks and some anecdotal stories to further help emphasize the information.

The information contained within is a snapshot of all the things I have learned through my mentors on how to be an architect in the today's market. I am thankful to be in a position where I am now passing this information down to you.

In addition to all of the great information contained within this book, I also have an extensive list of bonus material that you can download for free by going to http://www.architecturecareerguide.com/extras.

Introduction

I have a little secret for you. I don't know what I'm doing. Not really what you want to hear when you are trying to learn from me right? Hear me out. I know what I'm doing most of the time, but there are times where I get into a situation where I feel like I am over my head and I get that fear that I will be exposed as a fake. It may be that one moment when an owner asks me what I think of a certain design, or if the roofer asks me how I want to detail a specific connection. It's at these times that I feel like I really don't know what to do. But you know what? That's ok. In architecture we are constantly learning and if you're doing it right, you are occasionally getting in these situations and growing from it.

Here's the deal, when you first start out, you feel like you have no idea what you are doing. Your boss asks you to do something, and it's like he or she is speaking a foreign language. You feel like you should know all of this. I mean you went to school right? Well there are a lot of things that school just won't prepare you for. You know that feeling like you don't know what you're doing? It doesn't go away.

I have been doing this for over a decade and I still have that feeling. I might be in a meeting with a client and sometimes just wonder, "how did I get here?" Do they know that I don't know what I'm doing? What if I'm found out and they think I'm a fraud? This is normal and it is what leads to growth. If you are getting into situations that are just barely beyond your abilities, you will quickly learn to adapt and move forward. I know architects who have been doing this for over 30 years who will admit that they still don't know everything.

Granted, as you get further along, the moments when you feel like you don't know what you're doing begin to decrease and you can start to feel a little more comfortable. The best way to grow past this is to just learn as much as you can, as fast as you can. You could spend the next 10 years trying to figure out how this whole thing works, or you can immerse yourself in it and learn everything you can.

I've had to go through too many of these fear-inducing moments mostly because I never had anything to tell me everything I needed to know. I took professional practice classes in college, I read some of the handbook for professional practice, but there was never anything that spelled it out directly for me.

I learned what I needed to know through trial and error (a lot of errors), and through "on-the-job" training. I have been lucky enough to have some great mentors throughout my career that have helped me get to where I am today.

Your education beyond school is critical to your abilities as an architect and it is up to you to make it happen. Getting through this book is the first step in that process. Applying what you learn is the next.

But you can't start applying what you learn here unless you have a job to apply it to, so we will start there, Getting Your First Job...

Getting Your First Job

At some point you are going to have to get your first job in architecture, and I won't be the first one to tell you it's not that easy anymore. You really need to step up your application process and make sure everything is correct before you apply because you are now going against many other candidates who might be just as, if not more, qualified. When things got really bad during the recession, there were registered architects scrambling to try and get intern positions, so how are you going to compete with that? The good news is that times are getting better, and what you bring to the table can sometimes be superior to an experienced licensed architect. If you already have a job in architecture, that's great, you can skip to the next chapter, but it might be worth it to stick around to make sure you are setup to get your second job in architecture.

When to start working

You know you need to get your internship hours completed and you know it is going to take a long time, so starting work early does have its benefits. I would recommend that if you have the drive and determination, start as early as possible, even while you are still in school to get as much experience as you can, but I know for some people it is just not possible. Maybe you don't have the time or commitment to be a full-time student and an intern as well, or maybe you just really need to focus on your studies to make sure that doesn't fall behind. I totally get that, but think about it this way, when you graduate and you are applying to your first intern position, would that firm rather hire somebody who just recently received their degree and has at least a few years of experience, or somebody who just has a degree and has never worked before? In the end you both got the same degree and on paper you are exactly the same, except they don't have a sharp learning curve. This is not always the case, as sometimes your portfolio, personality or connections will still get you the job, but with the number of resumes firms see, you want to make the best case for yourself.

Another reason why I think it is good to work while you are still in school is that the things you learn at work will help you with school, and what you learn in school will help you at work. What you will soon find out is that architecture has two faces, the theoretical (school) and the actual (work). There are opportunities for cross-over between the two, but for the most part school teaches you to think outside the box, and work teaches you how to work in the box. But when you do these two together, you can think about your school projects and how they might be done in the real world, and when you are at work, you can apply the same kind of critical thinking you do at school. In the end you will have found a way to merge the two worlds and walk away with a system for design that has real world applications.

The biggest issue with working while in school is just finding the time to commit to both, and I will say that if you feel that you will not be able to give 100% to both, then you should not do it. Not learning from school or not performing at work is worse than not having experience when you are done. For most people however, you just need to decide what is more important to you and find a way to make it happen. Going to architecture school is a great time to make lifelong friends and really enjoy yourself. You will be creating memories that you will take with you forever and you will really learn about yourself. If all this sounds great and is more important to you than having a job, then don't start working early, but just understand it might be a little harder when you do get started.

Finding the right firm

Once you start looking for work, how are you going to find a job? Getting the job is the hardest part, and it becomes even harder if you are selective about the firms you apply to, but in the end you might get better experience. I want to briefly touch on the idea of shotgunning vs. focusing, or sending your resume out to every firm out there vs. only applying to select firms. At any point in your career, a job needs to be a win-win for everybody. You need to provide value to the company, but in turn, they need to provide value to you by fostering your growth, mentoring and making it an enjoyable atmosphere. If you are sending your resume out to every firm out there, the odds are not great that every one of those will provide value to you in the way you deserve. You might find a firm that is looking to hire you to just do menial tasks and never really help you excel, or you might find the gem that puts in the commitment to you.

While it is important to find the perfect employer, at some point you just need to get a job, any job, and that's when you start shotgunning. In a perfect world you can hold out and make sure that they want you more than the next guy, but in today's economy, it's probably not going to happen, especially at this early point in your career. You certainly don't want to be taken advantage of, but you are going to have to start somewhere, and that might mean you have to accept the offer from your number 2, 10, or even 100 choice.

So how do you even start looking for work? The first place is obviously the online job boards, because your best shot at getting hired is at a place that is actively looking for you. Go to Archinect.com or AIA.org and browse their listings, but it might be difficult because they are national websites and unless you are in a big city, good jobs might not be listed here. You could go to places like Jobs.com or Monster.com, but your search for architect will bring up a million software architect jobs that won't apply to you. The best place to start your online search is your local AIA chapter, if you have one in your city. It has the benefit of being specifically for architects, but is localized to your area and most of them have a jobs board that you can search through. Another way to use this is if they have a listing of local architects in the area, jot down the firm names and websites and start some research.

My typical research for firms goes like this:

1. Find firms that are actively hiring through job boards.
2. For firms that are hiring, read through job description and see if it is a good fit for the skills I have.
3. Find firm information regarding project types, size and studio setup.

4. If it might be a good fit, prepare my cover letter, resume and work samples, all tailored to what that firm is looking for.

If job boards don't turn up any good job prospects, I would then start researching firms. I would look up a firm's website to find information on their project types, firm size, location and culture. The "about us" page on most firm websites will give away a lot about the company itself and how they position themselves to potential clients. Do they list the firm staff or just the principal? Do they showcase events they have with the staff, or ways that they give back to the community? Does it generally feel like they are a good place to work? These are all important factors I look at before I even look at the type of work they do or who the HR person is. Once I have a good sense of who they are I will then look at the project types they work on to see if it is something I would be interested working on. Chances are if you are early in your career you may not have a good idea of what project types you might be interested in, so keep your mind open to the possibilities. After I feel that the firm setup and project types are a good fit, I will then see if on their about us or contact page they have a section for careers or some indication that they might be hiring.

Sometimes you might get lucky and find they are hiring and they just didn't post it on a job board.

Resume Tips

Once you have identified a good firm that would be a good fit for you, you're going to have to send in your application material. Usually this consists of a cover letter (or email), resume and work samples. There are all kinds of rules that people believe and your school counselor may have told you what needs to go into them, or if you google it, they will tell you the standards. Throw those out the window because you are not applying to a corporate business job, you are applying to a design firm. You need to stand out and be memorable and you need to showcase your talents in everything you do. But before we get into how you do that, first make sure you are not making these simple mistakes:

1. Typos and grammar mistakes
I'm sure you have heard it a million times, but double, triple, and quadruple check your resume, portfolio and cover letter/email for typos and grammar mistakes. I see this so often it still amazes me. I understand there may be the occasional typo here or there, but I shouldn't have to look past something to consider you. Not everything can be perfect, but there is no excuse for this not to be. Even better

than double checking it yourself, send it to a friend to read because sometimes having another set of eyes can find things you overlooked. Also, don't just rely on the computer to catch everything, because it won't.

2. Obvious Copy/Paste

I understand that you are probably applying to multiple firms, and it can get tedious typing the same thing over and over, but don't make me feel like my firm is not important to you. First, try to write every cover letter/email specifically to the firm you are applying to. Write a quick note about a project you saw on their website to let them know it is specific to them. Each application should be customized for the firm you are applying to because there shouldn't be that many. Using a shotgun approach may increase the odds of finding just one firm to hire you, but in the long run, it might not be a quality firm. The biggest mistake I see with this is when I get an email in three or four different font faces and sizes, meaning you obviously copied and pasted from other applications. Don't do this.

3. Not reading the job description

Architecture job titles can be confusing. What's the difference between a job captain, drafter, intern, and project architect anyways? It depends on the firm, and that is why you must read the description first. If you are just out of school, don't apply for the Senior Project Architect positions. Look for indicators such as years of experience, responsibilities and other requirements like degrees or licenses. In the end, titles don't really matter, it is about the work you will be performing, and you should take the time to make sure you can perform those tasks.

4. Poorly designed resumes

You spent a lot of time in architecture school designing buildings. You have put together numerous presentation boards, you obsessed over the layout of your portfolio, and your first impression to an employer is going to be a Microsoft Word resume template? Resumes are a one-page list of words, so you need to spice it up a bit. Take it as a difficult design challenge to make a boring resume exciting. I'm not saying to add a black background or full-page rendering (don't do that, it wastes my ink and I won't print it), but throw in some graphic design. Create a logo, have a consistent theme, add a highlight color. Do a Google or Pinterest search for graphic designer resumes and see how they do theirs for reference.

5. Too much/not enough follow up

This one can vary depending on the firm you are applying to, but in general you need to walk a fine line between how much contact you have with a firm. If they are advertising for a position and say no phone calls, don't call them. If you are cold-calling, one initial contact and a quick follow up a while later will suffice. You don't want to pester them, because that will only make them remember you in a negative light. On the same note, if the firm contacts you back and asks for more information or to schedule an interview, don't wait 5 days to respond to them. You don't want to make them wait, because if they have gotten to the point of talking to you, they will want to move quickly. Lastly, always, always, always, follow up any interview or correspondence with a thank you note. An email will usually suffice, but you have to immediately let them know you appreciate their time.

The Cover Letter

So with those easy ones out of the way, how do you go about crafting the perfect application package? First step is to craft your cover letter, and this isn't what business coaches might tell you. What I like to see in cover letters is a very brief (1-2 paragraphs) that highlight key items you want to show off that is in your resume, which can just be in the email and does not need to be anything formal. I put emphasis on brief because what employers don't want is to read your whole life story and how you came to appreciate architecture, save this information for the interview. You need to show me you appreciate how busy I might be and don't be a taker of my time.

The Resume

Now that you have the perfect cover letter that is specific to the firm you are applying, put together your resume. Your resume should be one-page, but for properly designed resumes, I don't have a problem with two pages. If you have a lot of work experience, I understand you need a second page and would appreciate not seeing everything crammed into one. But chances are at this phase in your career, you should be able to fit it all into one page. What goes into your resume varies by what your skills are and what type of firm you are applying to, but at a minimum it should include:

1. Contact information (name, email, address, and phone)

2. Relevant Experience - The emphasis on relevant, as I need to know how long you have been working in architecture or a related profession and don't need to know

about the waitressing job in high-school (unless it is somehow relevant)

3. Education - Short and sweet. What degree did you get from where and when? Include a bullet list of relevant studies or awards.

4. Skills - What computer programs do you know? List out your strongest first (or what the firm is looking for first) and go from there. You don't need to list every skill you have unless it is relevant.

5. Extras - What else will make you stand out as a candidate? Have you won awards or have been published? Do you know any extra skills that might be helpful (web design, welding, art)?

These are the basics of what you need in your resume, but what is most important is that they are combined in a concise and clear method that makes the information easy to find. Remember that the employer will be seeing dozens if not hundreds of other resumes, so if they have to search for your info, they will never see it. Also make sure you turn your resume into a pdf and don't send over a Word file or any other file for that matter. Pdf is the standard in the industry and you want to show that you are capable of understanding the standards.

Here are some examples of information on resumes I have seen over the years that I still remember to this day:

One resume was submitted that listed all the standard things I was looking for (architecture degree, knowledge of Revit, etc.), but they also stated that they were excellent at graphic designs and layouts. Normally I would look at this and mark it up as a bonus; except this resume was very poorly designed and showed that they didn't know the first thing about graphics. Obviously I couldn't trust what they were saying and I did not go any further with this candidate.

On the other end, I once received a resume that was short of what I was looking for. They met some of the requirements (Master's degree, Revit), but the candidate just didn't have any professional experience, and I was looking for a more experienced person. However, their resume was graphically appealing and it was easy to navigate. But the biggest reason I followed up with this person is because they showed some extracurricular work where they helped build schools in other countries. This showed me they had some experience in construction, but more importantly they were the type of person to give back, and that is something that fits right into our firm's mission. I scheduled an interview and hired them shortly after, all because they added that extra little piece of information that was easy to find.

For more information on what should go into your resume, go to http://www.architecturecareerguide.com/extras.

JohnSMITH

123 Main Street
Anywhere, USA
Ph|555/555-5555
Email | john.smith@email.com

Experience〉 **Job Captain** | 2011-2012
Jones & Associates
- Creation of **Construction Documents** for commercial projects
- Development of presentation materials for **Schematic Design**
- Model-making using various materials

Architectural Intern | 2010
Trendy Studio
- Participated in **design** of 35,000 sf Amphitheater
- Development of high-quality computer **renderings**

Barista | 2008-2010
Coffee Shop
- Customer Service
- Led Training Program for new hires

Education〉 **State University** | 2010
Bachelor of Architecture
- Focus on **sustainability** and **technology**
- Graduated with high honors
- **Award of Excellence** 2008, 2009, 2010

Skills〉 Excellent
- **Revit** | AutoCAD | Sketchup | Adobe CS

Proficient
- Rhinoceros | V-Ray

Awards〉 **Award of Merit**
Student Design Competition – 2008

Organizations〉 AIAS / President 2008
Tau Sigma Delta Honor Society / Member

Interests〉 Robotics, Woodworking, Computer Programming

1 Sample of simple and clean resume design. Download at
http://www.architecturecareerguide.com/extras

29

The Portfolio

So you have your cover letter created and your resume tightened up, now comes the hardest part, the portfolio. You have put in so much time and effort into your school work, how can you possibly show it all in one email-able pdf? You can't, because you have to make sure your email gets to them and a 50MB file is not going to make it, or if it does it will just be an annoyance for them. Most firms will actually tell you the file size limit they will accept, so make sure you show them you can follow the rules and send what they ask for. What many firms are looking for is a work sample, which is really just a short portfolio with basic information. This could just be a couple of pages, but show the type of work you perform and what the employer could expect from you. This is a teaser that will make them want to see more in your portfolio; it is just something to get them to want to find more. The projects that are shown in your portfolio should be your best work and should apply to what the firm is looking for. Tailor each and every submission to the firm you are applying for.

If you only send a work sample, how are you going to show the breadth and depth of you skills? This is where the portfolio website comes in. This is becoming more common, and I think it's a great way to get your portfolio seen. I appreciate when I see someone submit a link to their portfolio website because it gives me the ability to see their work, but it also shows me they are capable of learning something beyond architecture. The best part is you don't have to worry about file size, page limits or image resolutions and you can easily update it as needed. If you really want to learn how to catch up to everyone else applying by making a portfolio website, find a free ultimate guide at:

http://www.architecturecareerguide.com/extras.

The Interview

Hopefully after sending in your perfect cover letter, resume, work samples and portfolio website, you will be called in to meet with the firm. This is an exciting moment, but also a very nerve wracking one. The purpose of this interview is to get to know who you are as a person. They have already identified that you generally have the skills they are looking for, so now they want to make sure you are a good fit for the firm. They will ask you a series of questions that will help them gauge what type of personality you have and whether you will be a good employee. Most of the times the answers to the questions are less important than how you answer them, as what they are looking for is how you handle yourself in the situation.

The first thing to consider when showing them that you will be a good fit for their firm, is before you even show up, how are you going to dress? You definitely want to be professional and you don't want to show up in ripped jeans and t-shirt, but how much is too much? Thankfully with the prevalence of the internet you can do some quick reconnaissance and see what the culture of the firm is. If you did your research on the firm before, you should already have a feel for this, but look for pictures of how people dress on their website, or Facebook or Linkedin pages. This will give you a sense of how they hold themselves, are they laid-back or corporate? Once you have this figured out, always show up one level above what you expect. If everyone on their website is in jeans and a polo shirt, you can feel safe in slacks and a dress shirt, but you can probably toss the jacket. If everyone is wearing ties, you want to show up with a tie and jacket.

For the ladies, make sure you are dressed professionally as well, but I don't know enough about women's fashion to give you advice beyond that. In any event everyone needs to be confident and comfortable in their dress, and being a creative profession, it doesn't hurt to be fashionable as well.

When you get to the interview, make sure you get there early, but not so early that the interviewer has to stop what they are working on to talk to you, or where you are just sitting in the lobby looking around like an idiot. I always say that if you aren't 5-10 minutes early, you're already late. This applies to more than just the interview and should be something you keep in mind for life, don't make people wait, it's just rude. I'm a big planner, so if I know I have a big interview coming up and I am unfamiliar with the location, I will actually do a trial run if I have the time. I will look at the map and actually drive to the location to make sure I know how long it really takes (not what the map program tells me it will take), that I understand where the building is, and what the parking situation is. I know this may seem like overkill, but every interview is that important. Think about how many resumes you send out, and out of those how many have setup an interview? Just a few I would imagine. This is important and you don't want to blow it by showing up late and coming in with excuses already.

During the interview they will probably have a copy of your resume or work samples, but it doesn't hurt to show up with extra copies of everything in case they don't have a copy in the interview. They will constantly look at your resume and ask you questions that are obvious if they just read the resume, but they are not looking to find the answer, they want to hear it from you. For example, "I see here you went to X state school and you graduated in X." Clearly it says that on there, so they aren't looking for you to just say, "Yup." They want to hear, "Yes, it was a great program and while I was there I learned so much about X." The want to feel energy and excitement and that you are engaged in the conversation.

Many times the questions I ask are what I consider toss-ups, where I am just setting you up to give me a great answer, and all you need to do is say what I want in the right way and you win. But you would be amazed at how many times this doesn't happen. I might say, "Our firm focuses on sustainability and we think every building needs to be designed with this in mind, are you comfortable with sustainable practices?" Chances are I read your resume and I probably already know the answer, but what I don't want to hear is, "I suppose it's important, but I think the aesthetics of the building are more important." That may be true, and I'm not telling you to lie, but if you want the job, wouldn't you at least frame the answer in a way that answers with what they want to hear? Instead you could say, "I completely agree that buildings should be designed with sustainability in mind and can be a great factor in helping to form the aesthetics of the building. As you can see in this project that I did I focused on this exact aspect." There are many questions I will ask potential employees based on their level but for entry level positions I ask similar questions to many candidates, which I list below with what I'm trying to hear:

1. Walk me through one of these projects (from the portfolio) - I want to see how much you know about your own project, but also how passionate you are about your designs. Hopefully you love your work and can convince me of that, because if you can't even love your own work, how are you going to feel about our firm's work?

2. What are your end goals? Do you plan on getting licensed? Have you started IDP? - I want to know that you are in it for the long haul and you have plans on sticking around. I want to know that you hope to eventually move up and grow. I ask if you have started IDP because it shows you not only have plans but also take action.

3. Why did you choose architecture? - Again, passion. I want to know you won't hate work every day because you

chose a career that you don't like and are just doing because it's too late to change.

4. What do you know about our firm? - I want to see that you have done your homework and I wasn't just a check mark on your list of shotgunned companies. I want somebody who wants to work for me as much as I want them.

These are the questions I typically ask, but a lot of employers ask the same old questions that hiring managers tell them they should ask, so be prepared for these questions:

1. What is your greatest strength/weakness? - They want to see that you can self-evaluate, and are honest about yourself. You need to spin it into a positive like, "My greatest weakness is that I'm really passionate about design and I give too much of myself to the project." For me, this question doesn't help much because of the canned responses that don't seem personal enough to really get an idea of what type of person they are.

2. Where do you see yourself in 10 years? - Similar to the question about goals above, but not specific enough. What

are you supposed to say? At this point in your career, you don't really know what you will be doing in 10 years, but you might know you want to be licensed, so start there.

3. Why should we hire you? - Talk about making it an interrogation instead of a conversation! This immediately puts you on the defensive and sets you up to "convince" them to hire you. Just don't take it personal and talk about how your unique talents and skills are a perfect fit for the type of work they do and how you can bring a lot to the team.

When you are answering these questions, speak confidently and if applicable, give examples. This shows that you aren't just giving lip service, but you understand the question and can prove the answer to them. Also feel free to ask questions of the interviewer, because remember, they need to be a good fit for you and it sets the interview up as a conversation.

Towards the end they will most likely ask you if you have any questions for them, and the answer always needs to be yes. Come prepared with a series of questions that show your interest in them and that you want to make sure they are a good fit for you. Make sure it is a long list because a lot of the questions will be answered in during the interview.

Do research on the firm before and ask questions that help explain what you are looking for, for example you can ask:

1. What is the setup of the firm? Do you work in studios or divisions?
2. What is the culture of the firm?
3. What size is the firm?
4. How does the firm foster growth?
5. Does the firm encourage continuing education?

These all show that you are interested in how you will fit in and that you aren't just looking for the first place that will take you. Questions not to ask during the first interview are, "How much will I be paid, how many vacation days do I get and will I get insurance?" These are all things you can talk about later, but not during the initial meeting. Your first interview is like a first date, you want to make sure it is worth moving forward before you propose marriage and kids. You also want to make sure they understand you are looking to be a part of a team, but not just any team, it has to work for you as well.

After the interview, make sure you follow up the next day with a thank you email and that you enjoyed speaking with them. Provide any additional information you didn't have during the interview and let them know you are eager to hear from them again.

Negotiations

Hopefully you nailed the first interview and you are asked back for subsequent interviews. This is great because that means they are really interested in you and you are part of a narrowed down group of candidates. As you progress through the interviews and you are shown to be a good fit for the firm, you will eventually get an offer from them. By this point, you can feel pretty sure that they are interested in you over the other dozens or hundreds of applicants, and it can feel exciting, but don't get too eager.

This is a good time to make sure they really want you and get a little bit extra. They obviously want you, and they probably don't want to go back and start the process over again, so giving you a little bit more isn't beyond reason, in fact, a lot of times it is expected.

Don't get greedy though because you don't want to start the process over again either. The first trick to getting what you deserve is to know exactly _what_ you deserve. Look up salary reports, ask friends and do your research before you even get to this point and decide on what you would like to have and what the minimum you would take is. When the topic comes up, try not to be the first to offer up a number, no matter how had they press. A lot of times the number you would be willing to work for is lower than their offer. They know how much they are willing to pay; they just want to see if they can get you for less, so try to get them to give up the number first. If their number is what you are hoping for, ask for just a little bit more to see if they will budge. If it is low, let them know you appreciate the offer, but you feel this position with the value you bring to the firm would be worth more. You don't always need to negotiate money either, you can add in bonuses, vacation, insurance or other non-paycheck benefits. You don't need to go overboard, but don't take the first offer, because odds are they are low balling anyways.

Your first day

Congratulations! You are now employed in an architecture firm and the hard part is over, until you get ready for your first day. This can be just as nerve wracking as the interview. What do you wear? What time do you show up? Where will you be working? Hopefully a lot of this will have been figured out during the interview, but it can still make you nervous. Chances are your first day will be pretty uneventful as you are not ready to just jump right into production, but you should be ready just in case. Brush up on your computer programs and research the firm's current projects so you are prepared for anything. Most likely your day will be spent doing paperwork with the HR department for insurance, taxes, etc. and you will be learning their systems. If it is a good firm you might get a welcome packet or training material that will tell you all about the company standards and an employee manual that explains the procedures. If they don't review it with you, take time to read through it yourself to familiarize yourself with it. Eventually they might give you some small job to get you started and comfortable and test you out. Once they are comfortable with you on this, it's on to day two and then the rest of your career.

Architecture as a Business

Once you land your first job in architecture, you will soon realize that real-life architecture is nothing like the architecture you learned in school.

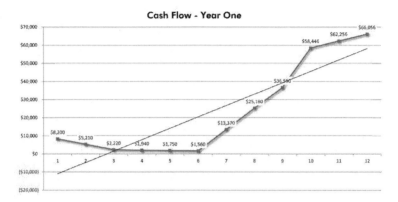

2 What running an architecture firm is really like.

Architecture is and needs to be a business first. While a firm's culture and their high design philosophies seem important, unless it was a profitable business, it will not be around long enough to keep that culture or high design. There are few designers out there who can make it in a non-profit world, so most firms need to be treated as a business first. By being a business, it means you need to work with a client, and working for this client means that you can't always just design things in a vacuum that have no regard for budgets or program or schedule, like many school projects do. You now need to worry about getting the design completed within a time frame that keeps the firm profitable, and you need to ensure that the design is within the owner's budget.

Budgets

The biggest awakening a young intern finds when they first begin working is how much a role the client's budget plays into your design. While it would be great to have the most extravagant design, without a client to pay for it, it doesn't exist. When the project first begins the client will come forward with a program of what they need and the budget they have to spend. There are very few open ended projects where the client will just find more money, because chances are by the time they come to you, they have already done their due diligence and know what they can afford.

Your first job is to reconcile their budget with the program and advise if it is even possible. A couple of ways to accomplish this is to use software or publications such as RS Means to aid in the construction cost for the project type and location, but more often than not, it comes from the architects historical reference on similar projects. They may have experience with this project type and can say with confidence what they think the budget will be. A simple back-of-envelope analysis might look like:

Typical cost per sf: $100/sf

Programmed sf: 10,000 sf

Est. Construction Cost: $1,000,000

Soft Costs @ 10%: $100,000

Owner costs @ 10%: $100,000

Total Project Costs: $1,200,000

We can quickly guess based on the typical cost per square footage number that the building should cost around $1,000,000. When we include some other variables such as soft costs (architect fees, survey, loan costs, etc.), and Owner costs (Furniture, Equipment, etc.), the total project cost can be estimated around $1,200,000. If the owner tells us that they only have $750,000 to spend, then we know there is a disconnect. We can then decide whether we need to reduce the size of the building, or the construction cost of the building. We will then analyze the provided program and see where some areas could be saved and also look at what type of design we can provide for less cost. Once we get to a comfortable cost per sf and building square footage number, we begin to design. As we progress through the design we will periodically revisit these numbers to see how we are doing in comparison to the budget. Design is an iterative process and is constantly changing, and if you don't periodically review where you are, you might end up with a building that is over budget and at that point it is a major ordeal to redesign.

Schedules

Another major factor in the design of the building is the schedule of the project, and we are talking about both internal and external schedules. This is one area that architecture school does give you a bit of a taste, but it is not exactly the same. You are used to having a time line to get your school project done culminating by the final presentation. The way this differs is that the time line is going to be a lot shorter in the real-world, and it is broken up into more milestones.

When the project first begins you will generally know when the owner wants to be in the building. Maybe it's a school and they need to be in before the school year, or they are a business that needs to be in before they change locations. Once you know the final date, you need to work backwards. You need to determine the construction time, permitting time, bidding and drawings. A basic schedule might look like this:

Certificate of Occupancy: September 1, 2015
Construction Time: 8 months (Begin January 1, 2015)

Permitting Time: 1 month (submit to City by December 1, 2014)

Bidding Time: 2 months (Open bidding by October 1, 2014)

Construction Drawings: 2 months (Begin August 1, 2014)

Design Documents: 1 month (Begin July 1, 2014)

Schematic Design: 3 weeks (Begin June 7, 2014)

Programming/Review: 1 week (Begin June 1, 2014)

What you find here is that everything is tied to each other and one little delay in any single phase can push the project back significantly. If you don't get your construction documents done on time, the owner might not be able to move in by September as they hoped. You certainly will build in some factor of safety for your time, but chances are, you will use every minute of your time.

What you also find is that of all the time it takes to get the project completed, the actual design portion might only be 3 weeks long. This is significantly different than the 16 weeks you used to have in school to get the design done. The majority of the time is spent figuring out the details, how to build it, going through all of the regulations and the actual construction of the building. This is an example of a small commercial project and would obviously be different for different sized projects, but proportionally, the amount of time designing versus everything else is the same.

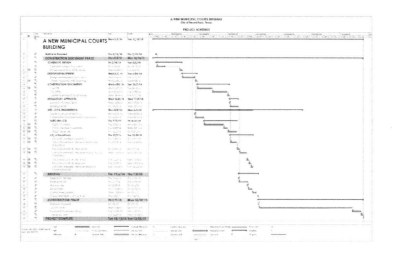

3 Sample project schedule created using Microsoft Project

Client Input

One of the biggest differences between real-life architecture and architecture education is the introduction of your client. When you are in school, most times you have an avatar client that you define, or your professor fills that role, but you are not dealing with a real client. Most times real clients aren't architects, are not accustomed to the process and are nervous about their money. There are times you might find the perfect client that knows and appreciates what you do and trusts you completely, but most of the times, they will want to give their input and want to know everything that is going on, and that is understandable, wouldn't you be the same way? As an architect though, you will need to learn how to deal with clients.

The first thing you need to understand is that you work for them, and they need to be involved in the project as much as they want to. If they "once considered doing architecture" and provide you with some "sketches" they did for you to base the design on, take that into consideration and really look into it. If they have a son who is good with computers and put together this sketchup model for you, look at it and ask them questions about it to understand the design. In the end, the owner is just as vital to the design of the project as any other team member, so let them be a part of the team.

The hardest part of the client-architect relationship is getting answers from them. Many times, you need to know which direction they would like to go in, but they flip-flop or they don't get you an answer, and a lot of times it's because they are nervous making this decision. If they take too long to make the decisions, it could throw off your design schedule and the entire project schedule, but in the end, nobody will remember that it was the owner's fault for not answering the questions in time. The best way to eliminate the obstacle is to make sure the issue you are trying to resolve is crystal clear and the owner knows exactly what they are being asked to decide on. If that means doing a computer rendering or even building a mockup, the more they understand the situation, the quicker they can decide. Many owners don't know how to read plans and they definitely don't understand archi-speak, so give them something tangible to base their decision on.

I once had a project to redesign a fire station in a small town for the previous, semi-retired Fire Chief. He was a great client and we really hit it off from the beginning. As I started putting together some basic designs based on what I thought he wanted, he started sending me some of his sketches. He says he was always interested in architecture and thus he would sit down after a long day of work and put his ideas down on paper. They were drawn in pen with white-out everywhere with pieces taped on, and while it wasn't what the best artwork in the world, he thought they were amazing, so I did too. As I sat down and looked at them I began to realize that what I was designing was nowhere near what he was thinking, and I began to redesign it. In the end I gave him a building that was similar in language to what he wanted, but had all the elements I expected to see in a fire station. It was a great moment of collaboration between wannabe architect and architect, and I couldn't have done it without his input.

Contracts

Since architecture is a business and not something you do for fun, you will need to use contracts for all clients. Most states also require you to have a contract on any project, whether it is pro-bono or not, to cover everyone, but you should always have one regardless. Contracts can be as easy as a one-page agreement, or a multi-page AIA document. The contract is intended to make sure every party knows what the expectations are from the beginning and how to resolve things if it goes south, which it could, even with your best client. The contract will contain language that says who is a party to the contract, what the scope of the project is, what the payments will be, and how disputes will be resolved. Chances are as an intern, you will not have a lot of involvement in contracts, but just know that they exist to protect everybody on the project and they must be used. To read more on contracts, take a look at the AIA.org website and see all of the different kinds they offer (there are a lot).

Consultants

Most architecture is not created in a bubble, and you will need the input of many consultants on the project. Remember back in architecture school that project where the professors made you work in teams? Remember how hard it was to get the other team members on the same page and following the same path? Now try doing that with people who aren't even architects and you will see what it is like working with consultants. Consultants can range from a simple structural engineer on a small project, to multiple specialists on larger projects. It is your job as the architect to make sure everybody is coordinated with your design, as well as with each other. You need to make sure you are keeping them updated on the design progress and their work is not conflicting with yours or the other consultants. On a larger project the list of projects could include:

Structural Engineer

Mechanical Engineer

Plumbing Engineer

Electrical Engineer

Civil Engineer

Landscape Architect

Technology Consultant

Interior Designer

Furniture Consultant

Acoustic Consultant

Roofing Consultant

Sustainability Consultant

Accessibility Consultant

It is critical that you are able to communicate your design to these consultants and facilitate the design team coordination. There will be many meetings with these specialists to resolve issues that come up between all the trades. You might need to ensure there is enough room in the ceiling for the HVAC, lights, acoustic panels, security wiring, fire sprinklers, data cabling and audio-visual cabling, and also make sure that none of their items run into each other. In any of the projects you did in school, did you ever have to make sure somebody else's design worked in your building? That's how you spend a lot of your time in the real world.

Your role is to keep all of the consultants up to date with the design by sending out updated files. These could be Revit models or CAD files depending on how your office works, but it is important that everyone is working off the same backgrounds. I have had projects come back from the Mechanical Engineer showing all of his ducts going into a mechanical room that was previously moved over to the other end of the building for structural reasons. This was completely my fault for not relaying that information I received from the structural engineer and the subsequent changes we made so they could update their drawings.

Another important way to coordinate this trading of information is to have consistent design team meetings with everybody in the room. This is the chance to go through everybody's scope and ensure that they are all talking to each other. We might discuss moving a wall out for aesthetics reasons and the structural engineer will recommend we go to a certain spot, to which the MEP engineer will recommend we tie their system into it, while the civil engineer will rework the grading and the landscape architect will move their irrigation in that area. One simple move by the architect sets so many dominoes to fall; that it is much easier to get everyone's input on the change before it is finalized.

Contractors

Once the project is designed and coordinated with the consultants the owner will bring in a contractor to build it, and now you have a completely new person you have never had to deal with. The contractor can be your best ally, or worst enemy depending on how your relationship is with them. If you start off on the wrong foot, they may throw you under the bus for your "bad design" that is causing all of these problems, where if you get along, they will make your life easier by working with you. For you, the construction administration portion is a major component of your project schedule and budget, so you probably want to make it an enjoyable experience. Remember that hypothetical schedule we put together earlier? You were spending 4 months designing a project, but you will now be spending 8 months as part of the construction process, and for you this will be 8 months of potential learning. We will go into depth on how to deal with contractors in the Construction Administration chapter, but for now, you just need to understand that being a part of the construction process can be more valuable to you early in your career than anything else you do.

Finding work

Unlike architecture school, the projects don't just come out of thin air, you need to find them. They can come from a number of sources like word of mouth or marketing efforts, but they don't just happen. You will end up spending the majority of your time as an architect finding the work that will help pay the bills, and this is something that you can't even bill somebody for! So how do you go about finding the work? Many medium to small firms will have a person or department who are solely responsible for the business development or marketing efforts, but in smaller firms it is up to everybody to do this. The most common way to find work is through your network of connections. Just like in any business, most often it isn't what you know, but who you know, so you need to get out there and get to know as many people as possible. But why would an intern need to know people or bring in work to the firm? It is because the fastest way to advancement and to prove your worth to the firm is to bring in work. It won't always happen and definitely doesn't happen quickly, but if you can show you are actively seeking out work or even bringing in work, you are more valuable to the firm, or have set yourself up to start your own firm.

There are a number of ways you can expand your network, with no two ways producing the same results, so try them all until you find your niche. The first place you need to look is your existing network, and the connections you have already made. Think back to people you met during architecture school that could need your services. Obviously if you only talked to other architecture students this will be limited, but chances are you met students in the business school, or real estate, or even that pre-med roommate you had. These are all potential clients that if you cultivate the relationship now, when they advance in their career, you are the first person they will call, and you get the added bonus of cultivating a great friendship.

Beyond your existing connections, you can start joining organizations that will expose you to others that are great connections. You could sign up for volunteer organizations such as Habitat for Humanity, the Humane Society, or tree planting for Arbor Day. All of these organizations will take time outside of work, but when the time comes, the connections you make could help you in the future. I'm a big believer that the more you help first, the more good that comes back to you. Call it karma or fate or whatever, but giving to others can help you in so many ways, even if only to make you a better person.

Politics

One thing I never thought I would be involved in for my career is politics and dealing with elected officials, but if you are doing work of any significant size, you will at some point need to deal with politicians. This isn't a bad thing either, because the more you embrace it, the easier it becomes for you in your career. If you are working on custom residential design you might be dealing with a home owners association or the city zoning commission. If you are working in education you might be dealing with school boards and city council members. Learn how these groups work and you will have an expanded team of individuals that are all on your side and help to move your project forward.

The way most groups make decisions is through the members of the group coming together and making decisions. This can range from a small group of elected officials to appointed staff. Regardless of the setup they all typically follow the same guidelines in that they must announce when they are going to meet to discuss decisions, and invite the public to comment, and will take a public vote on their final decision. Before it even gets to this point, there might be a lot of private conversations and discussions and "politicking" going on. The groups can vary in size, but are generally odd numbered so there are no split decisions, and they will all have an intentional focus, but the most common are below.

Home Owners Associations

If you are dealing in residential design, you will at some point deal with an HOA, as you will likely need their approval for design. The purpose of the HOA is to have a group of homeowners enforce the standards of the community via their covenants, conditions & restrictions

(CC&R's), which are something every homeowner who moves into the area signs on to. The association is usually made up of elected individuals that are homeowners of the area. These members will be from many varied backgrounds, with some members being part of the architectural review committee (ARC), that you will have the most communication with. You need to get their approval to build and they are looking for such things as, building style, building height, square footage, lot coverage and even landscaping plans.

School Board of Directors

For those working in the school district, you will have contact with the district staff mostly (facilities, principals or even superintendent), but all these people get their direction from the board of directors. While district staff is hired for their positions, the boards of directors are an elected group that usually consists of local community members. They make the decisions on when and where to build schools, what to remodel, and the budget for everything. They base their decisions on recommendations of other groups, but in the end the decision stops with them, so you need to make sure you have them on your side.

Planning and Zoning Commission

Planning and zoning (P&Z) is a group of members appointed by the city council to make decisions on how the city will be laid out so that they make the best use of the land. They will determine what types of properties can be built on all of the lots within the city limits as well as the design requirements for those buildings. They are not elected, but are appointed into their positions from the elected city council. They typically consist of volunteer members who are somehow involved in the planning, construction, or architecture fields. Many times people who serve on this commission are also looking to become an elected city council member in the future. As an architect you will have to deal with this commission when you have something unique about your design that may or may not meet their regulations, and you need to get approval for the change (variance) or an interpretation of the rule.

As an example I once had to present to P&Z for a building I was working on that didn't exactly meet the requirements of the code for the percentage of stone required on all buildings. The code stated that I needed 50% of the building to be of a natural stone, but our building was of a highly technical use that required a specialized facade surface, and add the fact that it was placed in the back of the site with another building in front of it. I felt that while the intent of the code was to have an attractive front facade for the public, this wasn't possible for my building, and by placing it far enough back from the public front, I met that intent. I presented my case to P&Z and we eventually compromised and I only needed to provide a small portion with stone, and didn't need it all the way around.

City Council

Cities and towns are typically governed by an elected body of members sometimes referred to as the City Council, who direct a City Manager to carry out the tasks. The council tends to have 7 members and in conjunction with the city mayor, they are tasked with making city policy, setting the budget and in general setting the rules for the city. They take recommendations from other boards and commissions, like P&Z, and make them official. In the council-manager setup, they will appoint a full-time paid staff member called the City Manager who will administer all the rulings the council has decided upon. This city manager will have their own staff to help them out in all different departments and roles. If you do a lot of work in the city, and especially if you do work for the city, you will get to know the council and city staff very well, as they will may be needed to make a ruling on your variances, or even approve your contract (if you work for them). They also set the policy on what city funded projects move forward, so if you want to do work for them, you should know what is coming out so you can get on the list to do the work.

The council will meet a set number of times a month in a public forum where everything is transparent and the public is allowed to comment. If you do work for the city, you will be at a lot of these meetings when they approve your contract, or when you give updates on the project, or on some occasions when you are showing off the award their city project that you designed won.

I have been to more council meetings than I can count, but for the most part they are all the same, I show up early and meet and greet the council and public who are there (always networking), then the meeting starts, and I wait, and wait, and wait. Since the council only meets a few times a month, there are a lot of items they need to discuss from policy on water, to transportation, to some local landowner wanting to change their residential zoned lot into a gas station (these ones always take a long time). They need to discuss all of these items in detail to make an informed decision, but for me, it is just something I have to wait through until they get to my item, which always seems to be last. By the time they get to my item, it is usually a short update or decision, where I might stand up at the lectern and show them images of the design, go over the current construction schedule and/or budget. I say thank you and I'm done, sometimes 5 minutes of talking for 2 hours of waiting, but it is necessary.

If you have never been, I recommend everybody go to at least one public meeting, just for the shear fact that you should understand how they work, but also to get out there and be a part of the process. You will at some point in your career need to stand up and talk about your project to a group of people, but unlike school, they may not know anything about architecture, and sometimes, don't care either. Just like getting comfortable speaking in front of your professors and guest critics, you need to be comfortable with speaking in front of a board as well, and the more you are around it, the easier it gets.

Business Management

Aside from all the previous items that show the difference between real world architecture and architecture school the hardest thing to learn is often the business management process that you will need to learn by doing. Architecture is a business, and unfortunately most architects aren't great business people because they have never been taught this. There are issues such as business entity type, accounting method, cash flow, human resources, insurance and forecasting that need to be considered in order to be a successful business. Firms need to decide if they will be a sole proprietor, limited liability company (LLC), or corporation, but this will need to be discussed with a professional other than myself to figure that part out.

The biggest concern in most firms is cash flow and accounting, because without the cash, you can't pay your employees, rent, or utilities, and you can't make any money without those items. When you get a project in the door, you sign a contract and start working on it. You get your consultants under contract and get your staff working on it as soon as possible, but unless you got a retainer, you haven't gotten paid yet, so how are you going to pay your consultants and staff? You need to float them the money until you get paid and that can sometimes take months. You should be sending out monthly invoices of the work completed to date to the client, and until the client pays you, this goes into accounts receivable, or money you know is coming, you just don't have it yet. When you buy something or contract for services that you haven't paid yet, this goes into your accounts payable, or items you know you need to pay but haven't yet. Hopefully in the end everything works out and your client pays you and you pay your consultants and everybody is happy, but this is rare. What if you client doesn't pay you for over 30 days, or 60 days, or even 90 days? How are you going to pay the bills you have, so you are not paying them for 30, 60 or 90 days? This is a cash flow problem. How you resolve it could vary in a number of ways, ranging from invoicing early, collections or getting a loan to cover the difference. This is all something that should also be discussed with the accountant the firm uses.

When you have more employees than yourself you need to worry about human resources tasks like salaries, insurance and employee manuals. You need to make sure you are following all the rules and are paying everybody fairly and you are taking out all the required taxes and offering health insurance. You need to make the employee aware of their options for benefits such as sick or vacation days, 401k, and overtime pay. These are all items that most architects have never had to deal with, and it might take hiring somebody in the office management position to handle if the firm is big enough.

Depending on the size of the firm and the type of projects they do, you will also need some sort of insurance. Some clients will require it, but most firms have it to protect them from frivolous lawsuits. You will need the standard insurance that will protect the business from anything that happens at the business, but you will also need to get professional liability insurance. This insurance covers the firm and any of its employees from negligent acts or errors and omissions in the performance of architectural services, or anything you messed up on the drawings that led to someone suing you. Some architects working on small project that are generally safe from lawsuit will forgo this insurance, or practicing bare, but working with an insurance agent could get them at least some sort of coverage, which is probably worthwhile.

One important aspect of the architecture business is forecasting which looks at potential projects and what could be coming in the future. This will trigger a number of critical aspects of the firm such as loans and staff levels. If you know there are some high probability projects coming in soon, you could possibly feel a little more comfortable about floating the cash for a while until they come in without taking out high interest loans. It could also tell you what is working, or where you need to focus your marketing efforts so that you have a good number of projects coming in throughout the year. Another important thing it affects is if you have the staff on hand to perform the work you have now and in the future. If you are barely keeping up with work now and have a lot coming in, maybe you need to hire on another staff member, or look at taking in temporary summer interns for short projects. On the other hand, if you have a lot of staff sitting around not working on billable projects and you don't really have any projects coming in soon, maybe it is time to take a look at changing the staff levels or shifting them to other tasks. These are all items that go into the decision to hire or lay off staff, so now you know why it might be hard for you to find that job, or why you were let go, as it is usually not an easy decision to be made.

All of the items discussed in this chapter come back to one thing, getting the work so that you can run the architecture firm as a business and not just an art studio. This is what makes architecture so different from what you were taught in school. While aesthetics and design are very important, it would not exist without that project coming in, without that client coming in the door, or you going out and networking, all things architecture school never taught you.

Identifying Potential Projects

What is the most important aspect of an architecture firm? What is it that is so critically important the firm would cease to exist without it? Is the culture of the studio, the mission statement or the people that work there? Is it the building you are in or the computer software you use? I'm going to let you in on a secret; it is none of these things. The single most important thing for an architecture firm to have is work. In order to be a business, the firm must have consistent work, and the way in which you get this work can vary depending on the type of projects you are involved in and how you market yourself.

The first important thing a firm must decide is what type of architecture they plan on doing, whether it is a specialized project or general project types. One thing most people don't understand, or understand only on a very basic level is that architects work on many different project types that can vary greatly. From houses to shopping centers to multi-unit developments, architecture can take many forms. Architecture firms can be generalists that work on many of these different types, diversifying their market, while others are specialists, focusing on one particular project type. These project types can run the gamut from interiors to skyscrapers, with the sizes of the firms growing accordingly.

Below are some of the most common project types architecture firms work on.

Custom Residential Design

A large majority of Architects focus their work on custom residential design work for single family residences. These projects are typically for a single client that is looking for an architect to design the house they will be living in. The architect will be brought in early on to help the client determine their needs, budget, size and type of building. The architect can be involved in assisting the owner in choosing a site, and selecting a contractor as well. Custom residential architects will design the building from the ground up, coming up with the form, aesthetics, finishes, appliances, sometimes down to furniture. They will assist during the construction of the house to ensure the owner is getting the best quality house for their money.

Other Residential Projects

As a subset of residential design, there are other projects that architects can work on from remodels to builder/developer design. Many architects will work on a residential remodel project at some point in their career, either early on as they are just starting, or for a family friend who needs help. Remodels and additions can be simple interior remodels to complex second story additions, and are generally a side focus of many firms and not the primary focus. Some architects also work on designs for a builder or developer who is building multiple speculation (spec) houses.

Multi-family

Increasing in size, multifamily is larger and sometimes more complex than single family residential in that it deals with larger buildings and developments. This can be in the form of apartment complexes or condo developments that house multiple families in the same connected building. These projects will involve more code requirements and planning department coordination and have to deal with factors such as parking, acoustics and floor-area-ratios (amount for floor area you can have on a given site).

Commercial Retail

These project types deal with projects from single building stores to mutlitenant shopping malls. These projects deal with more complex factors as parking, site flow, selling areas vs. storage and display areas. Specialists firms that are hired by large franchises will either be hired to do a "prototype" design that can be replicated numerous times, or can work for that one company only.

Municipal

This category is a mix of numerous project types, but all of them deal with a public client. This means that the owner can be a city, county, state or federal client. These projects have special rules set by the government in how the services can be contracted and bid out. Architects on these project types have to deal with numerous clients as it will be a board or committee that makes the decisions. Municipal work can take the form of a City Hall, Fire Station, Police Station, or Library for example.

Education

Education architects specialize in schools of varying levels from Pre-K, K-12 to higher education. Most architecture firms that work in the education sector are specialists in providing the right spaces for the students and dealing with numerous entities that have their hand in the use of the building. Each grade level has different needs and requirements that education specialists are experts in.

Healthcare

With all of the regulations and special needs, most healthcare designers are specialists in this field. They know about all of the specialized equipment, bed counts, insurance regulations and safety needs for these buildings and are best fit for this type of work. Healthcare can take the form of doctor's offices, hospitals, emergency centers and medical-office-buildings (MOB's).

Office Buildings/Tenant Improvements

Office buildings ranging from duplexes to multi-story skyscrapers have special needs. The number of tenants that can fit, the number of elevators, parking and rental rates are all key factors that are important for property managers. Architects working on this type of project need to be familiar with BOMA calculations (square footage calculations), demising partitions and acoustics. Tenant improvements is a small subset of this project type and deal with the interior design and changes when the tenants have turnover or change in space needs.

Other Commercial

Beyond these specialty commercial types there are many others that can't be easily categorized. Community centers, recreational facilitates, museums, hotels, art galleries, warehouses, and factories can all be considered commercial or even industrial and each have their own special requirements. Some architecture firms can specialize in just one of these types or add it into their portfolio of building types.

Getting the job

Once you have decided on the type of architecture you will do, it is important to have a marketing plan put together explaining how you will acquire these jobs. Do you go out there and get jobs by word of mouth, or do you use SEO to get ranked high on google searches? Do you join the local rotary club and meet the community or do you ask around to all your friends? What is most effective will depend on the project type you specialize in, where maybe joining the local education foundation board might help you with educational projects, or just asking around might get you custom residential projects. How you get the projects will vary by project type, location or personal style, but in general, your firm will find work by a client finding you (word of mouth), you finding the client (just ask), and a requisition process (RFQ).

Finding work by Word of Mouth

This is the best place to find your next project because it takes the least amount of legwork from you, and speaks to the relationship you have built with previous clients. The way word of mouth happens is: you do a good job on one project and that leads to a new project, it's that simple. Let's say you worked with a client to provide them with a custom house and you went above and beyond in servicing the client. You designed a great building that has all the details and design you would put into all of your great projects. As the new homeowner shows off their great new house, people will begin to ask about who designed it, to which your new friend/client will recommend they talk to you, their architect, and boom a new client.

This is beneficial to you because you have had to do literally no marketing to get the second client on the phone or in the door, and all it took was to do a good job for the first client. This sounds really easy, but you would be amazed at how many firms get this wrong. They sabotage their future word-of-mouth clients by being difficult to work with, way over budget or producing low quality work. If you do any of these things you may win the battle and get through the current project, but you are losing the war by ending the relationship there.

One of the best ways to make this work for you is to truly understand that you are working for the owner and have to work with them, not against them in the process. What I mean by that is when you are hired on, don't come in with an ego trying to prove that you know everything and the owner just needs to get out of your way, instead involve them in the process and get their input when you can. If they want to make a decision that you feel would negatively impact the project, think about it and explain why you think it might be a bad idea before immediately dismissing it. Ask them questions and give them options, and genuinely treat this relationship as if you will walk away with a friend at the end.

The idea of working with the owner also applies to the people they hire, especially the contractor. If the owner uses a traditional bidding method (more on this in Bidding and Negotiation), the contractor becomes one of the client's hired consultants, and if you don't get along with the contractor, it's as if you are not getting along with the owner. The same rules you use with the owner should hold true with the contractor too, don't think you know more than them, or dismiss their ideas. It's important to remember too, that during the construction process, the contractor will likely be out there every day and will be in constant contact with the owner, while you will only sparingly talk to either one. This breeds a relationship between owner and the contractor that you can't possibly be a part of, so you want to make sure they aren't conspiring against you. By that I mean if your drawings are poor, they will discuss this a lot. If you are hard to work with, they will eventually talk about it to each other. The last impression the owner might have of you is what they talked with the contractor about, so you want to make sure they are both friendly with you.

One of the most proud moments of my career came on a project I had been working on for a couple of years. Throughout the process I have gotten to know the many people involved in the team, and have genuinely gotten to know the owner well. As a part of our quality control and public relations efforts, we have a member of our team periodically check in and ask the owner how we are performing on the job. We have this come from a person not involved in the job to try and get some honest feedback on what we can do better, and we usually hear mostly positive aspects from the owners. On this particular project, when asked how I was performing on the job, the owner said that he is extremely happy with the process and honestly feels that even after the project is over, he knows he has made a friend for life. This is incredibly humbling and something I would say from my side as well, but to hear that the owner is that happy means that I have done my job right.

Finding the client

If you don't have the previous work or previous clients to use as a reference, getting new work will be a little more difficult and will require you getting out there. The best way to get work from a potential client is to just ask. Sounds simple right? Again, you would be amazed at how many architects get this step wrong because it is uncomfortable. It's not easy to go out there and tell somebody you need work and you don't want to sound like you are pestering somebody, but I have found the majority of the time you ask, the reaction is that they would have asked you, but <u>they</u> didn't feel comfortable! But it's not just a matter of asking anybody you see on the streets, you need to establish relationships or cultivate existing relationships first so that they trust you as a person before they trust you as an architect.

So where do you find these potential clients in the first place? Be where they are. Who are your clients going to be, a local business at a rotary club meeting or another architect at an AIA conference? While I still feel there is benefit to going to conferences and meeting other architects, if you are looking for work, your time is best spent meeting with local business owners or school staff, or homeowners. Identify who your client is first and do some research to see where they are, who they talk to and how you can get into that group. If you work on educational projects, for example, find out who is on the facilities staff and see who you know that might introduce the two of you. Join the local school districts education board, attend board meetings, get involved in your PTA, do whatever it takes to mingle with your crowd. Once you get to know everyone, it will make "the ask" easier.

"The ask" can be a difficult thing to do, but once you have established the relationship it becomes easier. Once you feel comfortable with the potential client, reach out to them, or if you see them at another event you both attend just start talking. At the right time in the conversation say something like, "So are you guys still thinking of doing that x project? You know I do that type of work. I'd love to help you out with it if you need." Chances are they might have been expecting you to ask, but they might not have even known. They may respond with, "yes we are still doing the project, but we already are working with x architects." At this point, it's probably best to stay positive and not speak badly about the other firm, but just let them know that if they need any help on this or future projects to keep you in mind. Make a mental note that maybe you asked too late and next time you should try to get in sooner and move on. On the other hand, the owner might say, "I didn't know you did that type of work, let's talk some more," and now you are in the door, on your way to getting the project.

Request for Qualifications

When going after large or public work, it is a little more formal, but the aspects you used in the first two methods also hold true. These project types will solicit to have architects compete so the owner can find the most qualified firm to do the job. It is a transparent process with many rules and processes, but a lot still happens behind the scenes that will help you win the job.

Getting a job through the RFQ process begins long before the actual project is put out for requests, and your job is to identify these potential projects early on. Through your contacts you have made through the second method, you will start to hear about potential projects before they come out, or you may see things happening in the community that lead you to a potential new use for a parcel of land.

Once you have identified these very preliminary potential projects, find out who the players are in the project and reach out to them, letting them know you are available if they need help. You want to foster these relationships as much as possible early on to not only stay in their mind when the RFQ comes out, but once it does come out, you aren't allowed to talk to them. If you have done the right ground work you will give yourself a better advantage to win the project.

Once the RFQ comes out, this is where your word of mouth processes come into play, as your portfolio and references will be a factor in most selections. While no two RFQ's are the same, almost everyone will require you to provide a list of similar work you have done and who was involved in that project. You want to show your best work and make sure you can get a good reference from the previous client, so make sure you have made them happy and the quality of the work is there. Selection committee's will call up previous owners and sometimes even visit the buildings to see the type of work you put together.

The reason it is called a request for qualifications and not proposals is that for most projects, they are not allowed to select architecture firms by the fees. This is to ensure that the best qualified architect is selected by their abilities and not on an under-cut fee. If they were to only base their selection on the fee, they might get an architecture firm that is not qualified to perform that type of work and will end up with a poor product in the end. This is why it is critical to be able to present your firms qualifications through previous projects and client references.

There is no typical RFQ, but their format might fall into a certain pattern of what they ask for. What they give you will be an outline of what you are expected to put together in the package and what the scope of the project will be. You will be required to format it a certain way (bound, no 3-ring binder, etc.), provide a certain number of copies and delivery by a certain time. This is to ensure that the group reading them will be able to review them properly and equally. You want to make sure that you follow their rules to the letter, because the selections are generally made by a group and anything that is off can cause one of the group to recommend you get thrown out. What is inside your response will differ, but they typically include your understanding of the project, your resumes, previous project experience and maybe even a schedule.

You show understanding of the project by explaining the unique characteristics of the project type and how you typically deal with them. You might say that you understand that the most important aspect of any fire station is response time and you resolve this by placing the bunk rooms close to the apparatus bays. This shows you really do understand the client's needs before talking to them and do so in a manner they understand. They don't want you to treat their project like any other project, so they want to know you appreciate and understand their unique needs.

Previous project experience is basically a sampling of your portfolio that pertains to their project type. You always want to put your best work in there, but make sure it is related in a way and shows aspects that can be similar to what they could use. I have won a lot of projects because they saw a project I put in the RFQ response that was very similar to the type of work they wanted and would fit into their needs already. They will often times ask you to provide information on the project such as the year built, whether it was on budget or on schedule and contact information. They will likely follow up with the contacts, so double check to make sure your information matches what the previous client say.

After you have submitted your response to the RFQ, it just becomes a waiting game as the selections will be made by a committee and it can take a long time for them to meet and decide. A lot of times, once they have reviewed all of the responses, they will select a few architects to interview, also referred to as a short-list. If you have made it to the short-list, congratulations, you are halfway there. They will typically take a few firms and setup interviews for you to meet the selection committee and present your qualifications. This is your time to make a personal connection with the owner and show how you are all about servicing the client.

You will end up showing a lot of the same information that was on your written response, but it is important to show your personality in the interview. They already know the information you presented, what they want to know is what will it be like working with you? They want to know that you really understand the projects you are presenting and that you will bring the same enthusiasm to their project.

There have been more than a few projects we have won in the interview phase because we told stories of the design process for previous projects or gave anecdotal evidence of how much fun we had working with the previous owner on the last project. Selection committees are often made up of people who are not used to dealing with an architect, and they want to feel the excitement of being one, which we provide to them by involving them, even in the selection interview.

Finding work by Internet

While the previous three methods of finding work have been the norm for decades, with the changes in society due to the prevalence of the Internet and social media, there is another way to find work, and that is by niche, expert and SEO. This idea starts with narrowing down your focus so that you are the pronounced expert on a certain type of architecture and in addition to word of mouth and networking; you get work via your website. This is a great way for smaller firms to compete against firms with a larger budget, but might limit you to the type of work you can do.

The first step is to niche down and step away from being a generalist firm. You need to find the one type of work that is being under-served or in high demand in your area. Maybe you specialize in rehabbing existing warehouses turning them into custom residential, or you are the specialist in preservation of mid-century modern houses. By niching down, it is easier to become the expert because that project type is what people will know you for. When that project type becomes available, there is just one person to call…you.

You have to be careful though because even though you might love mid-century modern and you could do a great job at it, what if you live in a small town with no modern houses in it? You might have to spread out to include other areas, meaning you will now be traveling a lot just to service they project type you identified.

Once you have identified the niche you are in, the next step is to entrench yourself as the expert on that type. Obviously the easiest way to do that is to have a portfolio of that work you have already completed, but that might not be possible. In order to establish yourself as the expert, you need to put on the persona of expert. You need to write articles in trade papers that give great information to potential clients, you need to talk to everyone you know about that project type, or start a blog focused on just that project. The more you are out there giving insight and information; people will automatically identify your name with that project type, creating the connection between you and an expert.

The last part of the step, SEO, is probably foreign to any architect, but in today's world, you should know it if you want to get clients. Have you ever wondered why when you search for something, the search engine always pulls up the most appropriate site within the first 5 results? The answer is SEO. SEO stands for search engine optimization, and in a nutshell, it is the method in which you ensure your website ranks higher on the search engine results page. If you have a website, you have to use SEO best practices if you want to rank higher and the higher the rank, the more people will find you.

The first step to SEO best practices is the use of what are called keywords. When somebody does a search online, the words they use are known as keywords. If somebody types in mid-century modern restoration (assuming that's your niche), you want to be on the top of that page. Once you have identified those keywords, make sure you use those words on your website in the title, headline and throughout the page. This will let the search engine know that is what your website is about and that you should show up when that word is searched.

An important aspect of your website is that you should not be using it as just a portfolio, but more of a communication tool. While people will want to see the type of work you have done and your contact information, what they really want to know more about is you. The days of an awesome animated flash portfolio website are over and users are past waiting through the loading page; they won't even wait to find your phone number that they can't print out anyways. You want to publish articles, or blog posts as they used to be called, which will let the visitor know more about you and your firm, and more importantly how you are an expert on the project type. You want to publish articles that relate to your niche, but are also SEO friendly for the keywords you identified.

Beyond your website you also need to have a social media presence today, as that is how new generations are getting their referrals and reviews. You need to be present, talking about your expertise and engaging with the community. Your connection with people through social media is very similar to the relationship in real world; people will trust you if somebody they know trusts you. They will hire you if somebody they know hired you before.

As an intern, you might not have the opportunity to take part in the first three methods of finding clients, but you definitely have the skills and abilities to find work by the

Internet and social media. Most big firms with interns have them run the blogs and update the website, maybe because they don't know how to work it or don't have the time, but your involvement can make you vital to the firm. If you can ensure they will get more work through these methods you ensure the firm survives, which is good for everyone, and if you can even bring in a client using these methods, you are well on your way.

All of this information on running an architecture firm as a business should be a part of the firm's business plan. To find out more on how to write an architecture firm business plan, go to http://www.architecturebusinessplan.com.

Initial Project Analysis

One of the most important phases in the life of an architecture project is the initial stages where you determine the program, site, scope, and project team. This one step can make or break a project and is critical for all the following steps. Once you identified the project and have worked through getting a contract with the owner, you now need to dig deeper into the project and make sure you understand what you actually going to do. It is also during this time, or even perhaps before this time, that you need to put together your design team that will be instrumental in the success of the project. You need to identify your internal architecture team as well as any consultants who will be giving input to the team. During these initial phases you are setting the groundwork for what the project will become in the future.

DESIGN AND DOCUMENTATION FLOWCHART

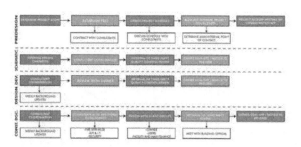

4Flowchart of design process. Download at
http://www.architecturecareerguide.com/extras

Programming

Any architecture project begins with programming in order to determine the exact needs of the client. This program is often owner provided, but depending on the project, you may be asked to perform this additional service. For project types like residential this can be as easy as determining the square footage of the home and any special rooms the client requires. You will already have a general idea of room sizes and what can fit within the required square footage, so you will be able to easily sit down with the owner and discuss this very quickly. For larger projects, this could be a much more in depth task involving multiple parties. In an office building, for example, you might need to determine the departments that will be in the building and the number of employees in each department. You will need to put together some typical offices and a hierarchy of spaces as well as any communal spaces such as break rooms and lounges.

Many large projects will contract out separately for this phase in order to put together a master plan or feasibility study, where you get an idea of all the spaces before they even hire on an architect for design. In another example, if a school district is thinking of doing a new high school based on their demographer's report, they need to know how much they need to build. They might hire on an architect to put together a report that will identify the number of classrooms, multipurpose spaces, number of restrooms, parking requirements, potential sites, square footage requirements and potential budget. Once the due diligence is completed, they might take this report to the board and then put out an RFQ for interested architects to do the design of the building, based on the report.

Even if the owner provides you with previously generated programming data, it is still important that you review it to make sure you understand the needs and discuss it with the owner. No two people look at a problem the same, so you might notice some things that could change or be more efficient, or you could learn of something different than you thought originally.

When you get the report, you need to check all the spaces listed and their estimated square footage requirements. You might find that the owner anticipated a much smaller space than needed, or that they doubled up on combined spaces. It is not uncommon to find that the owner or their consultant didn't take into account all users when they determined their restroom needs, and you need to add more stalls, for example. The point of this is not to pick apart what was wrong with the report, but to understand and clarify with the owner what their expectations are so you begin the project with the right information.

When you are hired for the programming phase, there are different ways to get the information you need, all of which should give you and the owner a final document to base all future decisions on. The first way to identify the needs is through a survey process where you ask questions of stakeholders, including the end users, owners, maintenance staff, or IT staff. You want to start off by identifying who the stakeholders are and request a meeting with them to get their ideas. You want these to be small groups so they can feel free to speak and you can have more advantageous dialog. This may take you more time by having to break it up, but you will generally get more input from the stakeholders. In these meetings you will identify the project and general requirements, and then open the floor up to discussion for what they need or would like to have in their spaces. For example, if you were programming a corporate office, you might meet with the accounting department and they would identify that each workstation will need to be at least 8'x8' and have plenty of individual filing cabinets in addition to group filing cabinets.

This might differ from the R&D department that will need a lot of bench surface with multiple power outlets.

Once you document all of the stakeholders and their needs you can now go through them and identify common items as well as special needs. It is also important to differentiate between the "needs" and "wants" so you know what is a minimum, and if possible what to add.

After you have a good idea of what each stakeholder needs, it is then a good idea to meet with representatives of each stakeholder department to review for any crossover spaces or conflicts between groups. You might find that two groups request extra-large conference rooms for their department, but neither will be using them all the time, so you can recommend a shared conference room between the two. You might also find that one groups request to have personal space heaters will not work with the maintenance department's use of an overall building management system.

One very effective way to get user input beyond the survey is to hold a stakeholder charrette, where users get to sit down and "play architect" for a little while. This is a great way to get user input on their needs and allows them opportunities to be a part of the process. In any large project you will inevitably get a group of people who will complain about the space or wonder why things were done a certain way, so this is a great way to ensure that they are a part of the design and understand why things are designed a certain way.

When you host a charette you want to either do it in a small group, or break them up into several smaller groups, so everyone has a chance to speak their mind. I like to have these charettes once for the bosses or higher-ups and once with the employees, as this allows for the employees to give their input without feeling they would be overriding their supervisor's ideas.

Another type of charrette that is beneficial is to also allow for public comment and input. If you have a controversial project or just a project that will have impact on the community, it is a good idea to allow everybody to have ownership of the project.

The format of the charette can vary by size or type of project, but in general you want to keep it to a couple of hours at a time so nobody gets burned out, and you want to put a cut off time so people understand that they need to not waste their (or your) time chit-chatting. You want to bring some ideas, whether they are sketches, precedents or just some pictures in order to get the conversation started and leading everyone in a direction.

Some people don't know where to start, so they might need a little probing from you. Ask them questions about their ideal space, or what they think of one of the pictures to get them talking at first. You will soon find that once a group gets going, you will have a hard time keeping up with their ideas. I like to bring plenty of sketch paper (bum wad, trace paper), markers, and even cut outs of typical space sizes. The idea is to have a discussion from a very broad point of view and to not get mired down in the details. Markers are great for this because it won't allow you to get too detailed in the design and forces the stakeholders to think in very broad terms. In the end what you are hoping for is some input from the stakeholders that will give you insight into what their needs are.

I remember one project I worked on that we had a very extensive programming and charette process involving many stakeholders and everyone with different opinions. The hierarchy of the company was such that many employees were afraid to speak up about their needs unless their boss wasn't around. I had many individual conversations with the end users and got some great insight. When the project was complete we had a grand opening ceremony where many of the employees even brought their families out to see the building. As I was walking around I overheard more than one employee pointing to a detail and telling their husband or wife and kids that they designed that part of the building. One of the more proud moments in my career was knowing that they felt they were so involved in the process they took ownership of the design and were proud to show it off.

Spatial Needs Spreadsheet

Room	Occ.	Qty	Size (SF)	Area (SF)	Notes
Entry Vestibule		1	150	150	Incorporate gallery
Public Restroom	1	1	80	80	Accessible from outside
Restroom	1	1	60	60	Large enough to use as changing room
Kitchen		1	200	200	
Serving Area		1	50	50	Adjacent to Kitchen, near service entrance for catering
Office	1	1	100	100	
Meeting Rooms	35	3	525	1,575	(15 sf/person) Expandable to incorporate 2 or 3 rooms into one); Various themes/sizes to incorporate uses as theater, game room; conferences
Storage - Exterior		1	150	150	
Storage - Interior		1	150	150	

Subtotals		
	Total NASF	2,515
	Non-assignable area (80% eff)	503
	Total GSF Required	3,018

Figure 2: Spatial Needs Table

In addition to the internal building spaces, the outdoor space will be equally as important and should include:

- Exterior patio large enough for 10-20 people adjacent to a built in BBQ/Cooking area and Bar.
- Open areas large enough for multiple temporary tents
- Permanent outdoor seating throughout site
- Permanent lights in trees throughout site
- Simple cascading water feature
- Near the creek will be a Nature Trail and new Fishing Dock
- Near the trail will be Bike Racks, Misting Wash Area, Dog Bag Holders, and a Drinking Fountain with Dog Bowl.

5 Spatial Needs Assesment

Define Project Scope

Now that you know what is going to go into the building, you need to validate the project scope. This includes not just the size of the building, but also owner budgets, schedules and internal conditions. The purpose of this is to ensure what you expected the project to be is actually what you are being asked to design. Does the program make sense? Is the owner's expectation of cost and time accurate? You need to validate all of this before you even begin to design because the biggest internal time and budget killer is doing work twice.

As you review the program you are looking for space square footages as well as building efficiency factors in their numbers. The program might include each space such as offices, break rooms, or lobbies, but what about corridors to connect them, the space the walls and chases take up? These are referred to as building efficiency factor and a lot of times are just a percentage of the total square footage. The more efficient a building is with less hallways or "wasted" spaces, the less this efficiency factor, but every project will need some sort of factor. You need to make sure what you are contracted for and expected to design to include everything in the building and not just the individual spaces.

Once you have identified the overall building square footage, these needs to be compared to the owner's budget for building construction. This can just be a quick double-check using a price per square foot where you take historical cost data and multiply it by the total building square footage. For example you might see that previously projects of similar size and scope typically had building construction costs of $100/sf, and your program has the building being 10,000 sf, which means the owner's building only construction costs should be $1,000,000. If you used a percentage of construction cost as your method of deriving your fee, how does this new construction number compare to your fee basis? If it's off, you need to discuss this with the owner from the get-go so they understand the discrepancy and they don't have an unreasonable expectation.

I have learned this the hard way before on a project that came in with a program from the owner and we based our fees on this information. As we progressed through the design process we soon realized that the spaces they actually needed were much more than we were informed, but were told to proceed anyways. As we got further along the design of the project led to much higher end construction which drove up the construction costs as well. By the time the design phase was over and the project was bid by contractors the construction costs were more than double what the owner had expected, and we were expected to redesign the project to get it within the budget. We were told we would not receive any additional fees for the re-design, nor would we get the fees we should have originally received from the first design for extra hours it took to design the bigger space with more detailed design features. If we had stopped at the beginning of the project and validated all of this beforehand, we could have designed the project the owner wanted within a realistic budget the first time and saved us the headache.

Just as important is to look at the owner's projected schedule to ensure what they are expecting is realistic. This is all based on the project type and size and will differ depending on the construction delivery method (see Bidding and Negotiation), and your experience and efficiency with the project type. You want to make sure the phases of the project you will be involved in are clearly defined and the owner understands what the deliverables are for each phase. You need to verify that you can complete each phase in the allotted time and how you will be presenting this information.

Clearly identify how you will get answers from the client group, and in what time frame they will give you approvals. There are times getting the owner and their group to approve you to proceed to the next phase takes longer than the design itself, so it is important to identify this process and factor it into the overall schedule. In the end you want to make sure the owner's schedule is feasible, and if not, discuss this before the project begins so they understand the constraints.

In addition to the owner's budget and schedule, you need to look at your own internal budgets and schedules. Using the contract with the owner and the overall schedule, you need to ensure you can meet all of the needs in the time and hours allocated. Given the architecture fee, you should know how many hours can be allocated for all internal staff by phase so you can track it throughout the project. It is important to periodically check the hours spent vs the hours allocated to ensure you are still completing the project in an efficient enough manner to not lose money.

At the beginning of the project you should put together an internal schedule that breaks the project down by phases and set up milestones for each. When you break up the project in more manageable chunks you make it easier to not get bogged down by the overall size of the project. This allows you to track overall progress as well as celebrate the completion of the phase. Rather than toiling away to the final deadline, you have a series of mini-deadlines that are much easier to focus on and accomplish.

PROJECTED HOURS WORKSHEET

Project Name									Project Number
Project Description									
			Projected			Actual			
		Hours	Rate	Total	Hours	Rate	Total	Diff	Rem
Programming	%	Principal	0	$	$	0 $	$	$	$
		Production	0	$	$	0 $	$	$	$
Schematic Design	%	Principal	0	$	$	0 $	$	$	$
		Production	0	$	$	0 $	$	$	$
Design Development	%	Principal	0	$	$	0 $	$	$	$
		Production	0	$	$	0 $	$	$	$
Construction Documents	%	Principal	0	$	$	0 $	$	$	$
		Production	0	$	$	0 $	$	$	$
Bidding Services	%	Principal	0	$	$	0 $	$	$	$
		Production	0	$	$	0 $	$	$	$
Construction Administration	%	Principal	0	$	$	0 $	$	$	$
		Production	0	$	$	0 $	$	$	$
Total Labor			0		$	0		$	

6 Projected Hours Worksheet. Download at
http://www.architecturecareerguide.com/extras

Getting the team together

Aside from very small projects, architecture is never accomplished alone and one of the most important tasks you can do for the life of the project is getting the right team together, both internally and externally. You want to have the right in house staff working on the project as well as the right consultants in order to have a cohesive team of experts filling their roles. You need energetic staff to do production, capable managers to run the project and expert engineers to all come together as one unit with the same end goal in mind of creating the best project possible.

Internally you want to make sure you have the appropriate staff levels to work on this project and to do it in an efficient yet quality manner. Depending on the project size, the design and production phases can run for a long time, so you want to make sure nobody gets burned out working on the project by being overworked.

Managers will identify staff that has previous experience in the project type or production task and place them appropriately. Good managers will also allow junior staff to have experience in many different areas so they can grow as well as have an opportunity to show their abilities. If you find that you are consistently doing the same task, such as door details or toilet elevations, and are not being exposed to any other aspects of the project, speak to your supervisor and let them know you are eager to learn other aspects of the project and ask if they could find a way to fit you into other areas.

The way in which architects select their group of consultants can vary depending on the project type, but in general most firms have a pool of engineers they consistently work with. If you already know what to expect and are already comfortable working with them, it is much easier to just use them. There are also times when you might need to bring in a different set of consultants due to the specialized project type, project size, or by owner request. Regardless of who is on the team, it is important to bring everybody in as a team from the beginning so everybody has input from the start.

At the beginning of the project it will be beneficial to have a project "kick off" meeting internally and with all design team members. This can take the form of an informal meeting with the architecture staff to explain the project and who will be working on what, to a formal meeting with the engineers to explain everybody's role and tasks. If a kick off meeting doesn't formally happen when you begin a project, it is important as an intern to make sure you get this information from the beginning. Identify what your supervisor's expectations of you are, what tasks you will be working on and how many hours are allocated. This will set you up for success by knowing each and every task you will perform, as well as a metric to make sure you are meeting the needs. If you are asked to be a part of the initial meetings with the consultants a lot of terms they use and discuss about the project might go over your head, but just take mental notes and look it up or ask your supervisor about it later.

Consultants

Your initial meeting with the civil engineer might involve a discussion with the project scope and site evaluation. They need to know the size of the lot, the location of the lot, existing utilities, parking requirements, or special features of the site. They will need an existing survey and you might come up with some general ideas of where the building will sit, as well as the grading around it to ensure you are placing it in a good spot. You will discuss general requirements of permitting and platting based on the location or existing jurisdictional information in order to determine who the engineer will need to submit drawings to. They will likely want to know if you or the owner are aware of any existing utilities on the site or any other existing features or structures, as well as what the owner requirements for parking might be beyond the city requirement.

Meeting with the structural engineer will help to determine the general scope of the project in terms of building height, general structure type, soil conditions or special loads. They will need to know if it will be multiple stories or have any special features such as a tower or monumental design in order to give a recommendation on the structure type. You might discuss the options for the different structure types and the feasibility of each. They will need to know of any special soil conditions and if the owner has contracted to have a soils engineer test the area to determine if it is made up of clay, sand, silt or bedrock. The location of the building might also add special loads such as wind, seismic or snow loads, all of which the engineer will need to know ahead of time.

The mechanical, electrical and plumbing engineer will want to discuss the expected or recommended HVAC systems, existing site utilities and occupancy type. They will discuss whether the project warrants simple "split systems" or if it will need centralized chilled water plant and what the ramifications of each are. They will want to know what is existing on the site and whether they will need to be on propane or natural gas, if the site slopes as needed for plumbing runs or where the electrical lines come from. They will also want to know the occupancy type in order to provide the right HVAC system for the usage, as well as any compartmentalization and zoning required.

It is also important for these three main consultants to speak with each other to make sure they are coordinated as well. For example, the civil and MEP engineer need to make sure that the plumbing lines or electric lines are connecting at the same spot on the site, or the MEP and structural engineer need to make sure that the structural system allows enough room for their HVAC systems. You will also likely need to coordinate with the landscape architect, interior designer or any number of other consultants involved in the project. It is critical to get everybody started on the same page so that they are all working together on the same goal.

Site Analysis/Existing Conditions

Even though you will be working on the building design, you will also need to be aware of and informed on the proposed site. The owner may already have a site selected, or may lean on you to help with the selection. They will want your input on lot size, building placement, zoning, or utilities, in order to make an informed decision. Once the site is selected, there are a few things the owner will be responsible for. In most cases the owner will be responsible for providing a survey and soils report. This information is critical to the engineers and in the end will help to inform your design.

The survey is a document that will identify site components and locate specific features of the site that need to be accounted for. The survey is done by a third party company that is typically hired by the owner, who will then forward the information to you and your design team. The survey will identify the extents of the lot to the property line and indicate the lot name. One important aspect of the survey is also the topography of the site, which will be in the form of lines running across the site broken in up in increments, usually one foot increments. This will tell you how the site changes in height throughout and will help you understand where the water will run if it rains, and how you will need to re-grade the lot to get a level building on it.

On the survey will also be the location of all trees that have been identified on the site. They will notate them by number and will provide a chart indicated the size and breed of tree as well as metal tags nailed into the tree with the number. This is important to make sure you are aware of any trees that need to be removed or relocated and which trees will need to be designed around.

The last item on the survey that will have effect on your building design is the location of the utilities such as electricity, water and wastewater. This will determine where you put mechanical closets or electrical panels in the building and will need to be coordinated with the engineers.

The soils report is another component that the owner typically contracts out to a third party company who will provide a report to you. The purpose of this report is to identify what the subsurface ground conditions are on the site and what type of foundation you should use for this specific location. Usually this will happen after you have already generally located the building so the geotechnical engineer knows where to check.

The way in which they identify the soil condition is by drilling down to a certain depth and logging what they see as they go down. They might find that the first few are made up of organic soil, with the next number of feet consisting of sand, silt, clay or even bedrock. This is important because depending on how far down bedrock is, or what the soil consists of will drastically change the foundation.

I have had projects in completely clay locations where we had to use piers with grade beams, which consisted of drilling down 10 feet with a 3 foot diameter hole and filling it with concrete, with all of these piers connected with concrete beams. Underneath the beams were carton forms, which consisted of pieces of cardboard that would decompose and leave a void under the beam, allowing the clay to expand when it gets wet without putting pressure on the foundation.

On another project just a few miles away we had so much rock below the surface it was cheaper to pour a flat slab of concrete and actually go up with the concrete than to try and dig down through the rock. With these two contrasting soil conditions so close together, you never know what you are going to get, so it is a good idea to get a soils report at the beginning.

Field Measures

Depending on the project, part of the existing conditions analysis is to verify any existing structures that you will be working around, adding onto or remodeling. Chances are good that if your firm works on this type of project, you will be the one out there at some point to perform the field measure, also referred to as an as-built. This is a task often delegated to junior staff, but it is also a great opportunity to get a real understanding of the building and what you are working with from the beginning. There are a few tips and tricks to performing a field measure efficiently and accurately which will depend on the number of people working on it and the technology available.

Many firms find it is easier and more efficient to send at least two staff members out to measure an existing building, while others only send a single person. If you are working in teams, it is best to organize it so that one person is responsible for measuring and the other person logging. This ensures nothing overlaps or is missed and helps everyone to focus on just one task. The person logging can either do it by hand, or even bring a laptop to input it directly into the computer, saving valuable time and mistakes of measurements that don't line up. If you are lucky enough to have more than two members, you could have the same setup, but have the third person in charge of photographing and documenting special conditions.

For many small firms, field measures are performed by a single person, which can add to the difficulty. You do not have somebody else there to verify you got everything, remember certain conditions or just have somebody to talk to when you are out on a boring field measure for hours on end. If you are out on your own, you could input everything into a computer, but I find it hard to draft and measure at the same time, so I carry around a clipboard with the floor plan printed on it to mark my measurements on.

I like to break my measures down to small tasks to make sure I catch everything. I start my measurements by going through the entire building and comparing it to the floor plan to notate any major discrepancies first, then taking overall large measurements. I will then start the measure the walls, doors and windows starting at the entrance of the building and work around the building going in a counter-clockwise motion, which helps to make sure I'm not jumping around.

As I progress through the spaces I will turn on the lights of the space I am measuring, which gives me a quick indication if I have measured a space yet. The measure itself can be done with a tape measure or a laser if you have it, but either way, I try to get things to the nearest 1/8" because in some cases you might need that 1/8" to meet ADA, and you have an accurate device, you might as well use it. Once I have made my way around the building I will be back at the entry and I will then proceed to go through and photograph every space, turning the lights off as I go to make sure I hit every space.

The notes and photos you take during the measure will be the best thing you ever do for when you get back to the office and start inputting the measurements. As much as we think everything worked out and we got everything located, you will find you miss something and you will need to reference your notes or photos. Having a photo that helps answer the question could save you another trip out to the building to re-measure. You can never take too many photos. If you missed a measurement of a wall, but have a photo that shows the room has 24"x48" acoustic tile ceiling, you can just count the tiles and get a general measurement. If you don't remember if there was one or two doors in the space, take a look at the pictures.

Depending on the scope of work, you will likely have to visit the existing building to measure and validate the floor plan, but you may also need to validate the reflected ceiling plan, the electrical locations or even existing furniture and finishes. If you are measuring the ceiling you will need to identify the ceiling type and locate light fixtures, sprinkler heads or exit signs. If the ceiling has an access panel or is a lay-in ceiling, you might want to poke your head into the ceiling and even take a photo to identify any special features above ceiling.

To locate electrical fixtures, you need to get a general idea of the location of power outlets and whether they are duplex or quads (two or four plugs). You will also need to identify the locations of the data or phone outlets and any switches. The measurements for these electrical fixtures don't need to be exact, but it will be faster to generally locate them based on the basic location on the wall and heights. Existing furniture and finishes verification could be to identify built-in millwork, or if a room has wallcoverings, carpet tile, vct or wood floors, etc.

The importance of initial project analysis

All of this work you setup beforehand will help you in the long run. By validating or creating the program you are getting a good picture of what the owner really wants and whether you are expecting the same things. It will help you make sure the owner understands the realities of the project and what is or is not possible. By setting the team up early and getting the conversation started, you get everybody working together collaboratively towards the same goal, and by analyzing the site and existing conditions you know what you are getting into before you start the next phase, designing.

A copy of the project information form is available at http://www.architecturecareerguide.com/extras.

Initial Designs

If you have made it this far into the life of the project, congratulations, you are now ready to do what you have been taught for many years in school, design. We have spent anywhere from two to six years learning how to design and we are finally at the point that we get to do that. We have identified the project, received a contract to do the work, met with the owners and analyzed the site, we now get to sit down and design the building. This is by far the most enjoyable part for most architects as this is why most of us got into architecture in the first place. Take your time and cherish it because it doesn't come as often as you think. As an intern you may not get the chance to design for a while because the opportunity doesn't come up often and a lot of times the principal doesn't want to give up this task. In really good firms the principals acknowledge the fresh talent and will turn over certain design tasks to junior staff, so take advantage of any opportunity you get.

Schematic Design

The first true phase of architecture design is the schematic design phase where you will put together the basic layout of the spaces, introduce the general form and language of the building, and begin the discussions of the systems in the building. You will be working with your design team and the owner a lot as you will be continually be coordinating to ensure you are on the right track before you get too far into the design. This phase is a basic starting point where you try different options and go through the iterative process to get a good foundation for the final design. Later on the design will be refined, but the point now is to just get a general feel for what the project wants to be.

To begin the design process you need to take all of information acquired during the initial project analysis and put it together graphically. The portion of the initial project analysis that you will be most reliant on is the programming document, whether a basic list of spaces from the owner, or a fully detailed package you generated. You need to take this verbal narrative and spreadsheet of spaces and put it into the beginning building block of design, the bubble diagram. The purpose of the bubble diagram is to get a general arrangement of spaces, their basic size and their relationships to each other. You want to indicate what spaces are required by floor by drawing a bubble to represent each space, with each bubble proportionately representing the size of the space in relation to the adjacent spaces. You also want to indicate which spaces need to be directly adjacent, semi-adjacent or visually adjacent to each other and which spaces need observational control over others. The bubble diagrams are a quick layout of the spaces to make sure they are all represented and that they can work in relation to each other, and also will give you a general idea of the form of the building. Whether all of the spaces need to radiate around a central space, or if they will be a linear L-shaped building will be determined once you understand how they all work together.

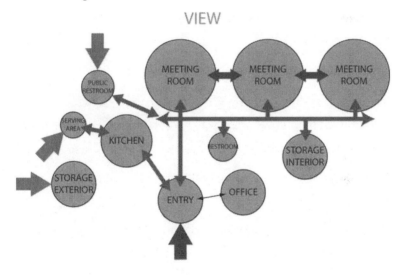

7 Bubble Diagram Sketch

The bubble diagram can also help to locate your building as you add more information into it. You might want to indicate which direction the views are, where north is (to locate the sun path), or where public access connects. You can get a general idea of the footprint and whether you might need to have more than one story, and if so, where the elevator and stair access need to be. You might also find areas that could have crossover functions and could be reduced to a single, larger multipurpose space in lieu of two smaller divided spaces. In the end the bubble diagram is a quick sketch that can give you many ideas on how to proceed with the design and if everything you need is possible.

This early phase is also a great time to get the owner, users, or community involved to facilitate their "ownership" in the design. It's very easy to print out some quick proportional bubbles, or even squares with general room sizes, and hand them out to anybody involved in the charette and ask them to put them together how they see fit. You will be surprised at the creative responses you get from the group, and if you present it as a no-wrong-answers study everyone will have fun helping to design the building. I like to take a laptop with me and while they are coming up with ideas, I will put together a basic model of what they are discussing, and by the time they are done, I have a cool 3d model of their ideas, which is a big hit with the users.

Once we have a general idea of the overall size of the building and what type of footprint we are looking at, we need to put it together in something that resembles a building. The method people use for this varies by architect, but many architects will start with the floor plan based on the bubble diagram and move from there, but I don't really like to work that way. I take the bubble diagram to get a very basic footprint of the building, then look at it in section and elevation, then go back to refine the floor plan. I like to work in all three dimensions at once because I don't like to let one portion of the building (plan, section or elevation) to dictate what the rest of the building will become. I think that all three dimensions need to be used to provide direction for each other. This will give you a better coordinated design that doesn't just look like an extrusion of the floor plan, but again, every architect is different.

While getting all the technical needs of the building into a form through plan, section and elevation, you also need to focus on the feel of the building. This is what I think separates architects from non-architects such as engineers or builders, in that anybody can ensure you get all the required spaces to fit into the provided budget and loads, but it takes a true designer to give it a sense of space.

Cheap tract homes have all of the same general spaces as a Frank Lloyd Wright prairie home, but the differences between the two could not be greater. One has all the rooms you need in a house, has all the right plumbing and electrical needs, the other has the same needs, but makes you feel warm and comfortable and just generally feels better.

It is important to this phase that you are thinking about this because you don't want to focus so much on meeting all the technical needs to forget about all of the emotional, psychological and sociological needs the building provides as well.

I think it also beneficial at this point to have many 3D study models that you can review and use to discuss options with. Whether this is in the form of computer models or physical models depends on your time and skills, but it is important to look at the building in three dimensions to get a real feel for the design. It is also beneficial when meeting with the client because they are not always able to read 2-dimensional plans and may need to actually see something to understand it. You don't need to put too much detail into these models at this time as their real purpose is to only study the form and layout.

If you are building real physical models these study models could be very simple and adjustable. I like to build study models using foam core and thumbtacks because it is easy to cut and stick together. As I try different forms and combinations I can easily remove the thumbtack and move things around or tack on another piece. Another way to do this is to use chipboard or cardboard and masking tape. As you progress through the design you can take these pieces apart to use as a template for a more finished model made of basswood or other finished material.

If you are more comfortable using a computer you could do the same quick study, but you want to use software you can quickly make changes in, and this will depend entirely on you. You're probably hoping I tell you to use this software vs. that software, but it doesn't really matter what you use, because the computer program is just a tool to get your ideas across.

If you are better at Sketchup than you are at Revit, then use Sketchup. If you are better at Maya than Rhino, use Maya. But get your ideas down and use them to refine the design. When you are using a computer, you need to come up with creative ways to involve others in the process. It is not as tangible as a physical model that the owners can pickup and look around, so you need to figure out how to get the same effect. Take a lot of screen shots from multiple angles or do a video walkthrough. If you have the technical skills do a virtual reality or augmented reality presentation where the owner can virtually walk through the building. Whatever you do, be sure you can use your model to spark discussion or refine your design.

You could also use a combination of computer and physical models, which is becoming more common place in many architecture firms now. Many firms are now contracting out or even purchasing 3D printers directly. The prices are now reasonable enough that you can quickly take your computer model, hit print and get a 3D print out of your design which you can use to study just like you would a manually built model. It is also relatively cheap and easy to send out your model cuts on a laser printer and assemble the model that way. These methods take a bit more planning ahead of time so that you can get your prints or laser cuts back with enough time to clean and assemble, as any architecture student will tell you.

Some of the most impressive presentations I have seen are the ones that use a combination of all of the above. An existing site plan built out of basswood with multiple options for the building 3D printed to pop in and out of the site model allows for physical involvement of switching between ideas. Augmented reality presentations that allow the owner to hold up their tablet and see their building in the actual spot are incredibly impressive and can win over a lot of clients. For the gamers out there, you could incorporate gaming consoles and software such as the Unreal Development Kit (UDK) to input your model, hand over an XBOX remote to the owner and let them walk through your building. Any of these ideas are all impressive and are on the current forefront of technology, but remember that in the end, the purpose is to get involvement and to improve your design.

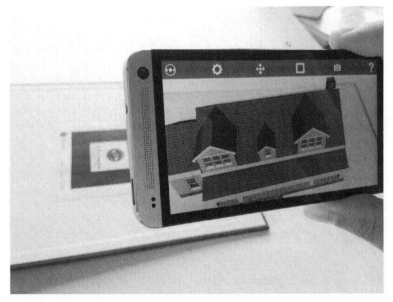

8 Augmented reality presentation

At the end of the Schematic Design phase you should be able to hand over to the owner a package that includes all of your initial project analysis and the basic documents for design. You want to have a basic floor plan with all the spaces identified with their general area or dimensions, as well as an overall building elevation on all four (or more) sides with basic materials called out. Sections and key enlarged areas can be included to indicate the basic layout of the building and more descriptive components. The package will also include an overall site plan, graphic representations and/or renderings.

SCHEMATIC DESIGN CHECKLIST

☐ ARCHITECTURAL SITE PLAN	
☐ PARKING COUNT AND LOCATIONS (INCLUDING ADA)	
☐ OVERALL FLOOR PLAN (1/8" = 1'-0")	☐ OCCUPANCY SEPARATIONS
☐ DOORS	☐ FURNITURE LAYOUT
☐ WINDOWS	☐ STAIRS / ELEVATORS
☐ MILLWORK	
☐ ROOF PLAN	
☐ EXTERIOR ELEVATIONS	☐ EXTERIOR FINISHES / MATERIALS
☐ FIXED OR OPERABLE WINDOWS	☐ EXTERIOR LIGHTING LOCATIONS
☐ DOORS	☐ ROOF PROFILE AND MATERIALS
☐ OVERALL DIMENSIONS	☐ INTERIOR ELEVATIONS
☐ OVERALL BUILDING SECTIONS	
☐ OVERALL DIMENSIONS	
☐ EXTERIOR WALL DETAIL	
☐ INTERIOR FINISH / LIGHTING / SIGNAGE NARRATIVE	
☐ SPECIALTY ITEMS NARRATIVE	

9 Schematic Design checklist. Download at
http://www.architecturecareerguide.com/extras

Design Development

Now that you have an idea on the form, feel and spaces within the building you need to further validate that your design will work. You will be spending a lot more time with your engineers & consultants to discuss systems and less time with the owner discussing technical items. Some owners might want to be involved in this, but in my experience, a lot of owner's get bored when you start talking about system components, HVAC, plenum clearances or any technical jargon they might not understand. This is the beginning of a lot of the behind the scenes part of architecture where you are researching and detailing.

One of the first steps you need to take in this stage is to meet with you engineers and go through your design and requirements. You will be meeting with the structural engineer to get their input on the design and make sure it is feasible, as well as discuss how to best achieve the results. You will discuss construction type and whether it would better to be built out of steel or masonry, or if you need to rethink the 20 foot cantilever you designed. The MEP engineer will give input on how to best provide a comfortable space given your layout, square footage or zoning requirements, and whether that is best served by a different kind of system. Chances are at this point you will already have discussed many site related issues, but now is the time to revisit anything.

The location of the building on the site will need to be coordinated with the civil engineer to ensure all of their systems will still work. You will need to verify the grading plan and ensure that water is not being directed into the building and you also will not need extensive foundation for a steep slope. Coordination will take place to locate any hardscape such as sidewalks and driveways in relation to the building as well as ensuring the parking lot is laid out properly. There will also be coordination between the civil and MEP engineers to locate the utility locations and where they will tie in together. Generally as a rule of thumb the civil engineer will handle everything from 5 feet of the building out, and the MEP will be responsible for everything from 5 feet of the building in.

Once you have the building generally sited on the lot, you will want to coordinate with the geotechnical report to ensure that where you are putting the building will work with the structural system proposed. If the geotechnical engineer hasn't drilled yet, this is the time you want to identify the location of the building so they can take some borings to prepare the report that the structural engineer will use to design their foundation system. This report will also typically include recommendations from the engineer that will identify the best possible foundation system as well as other options. These are all things you should discuss with the structural engineer for the impact on the building as well as the owner's budget.

When coordinating with the structural engineer you need to make him aware of any special features of the building such as extra heavy loads for storage or large assembly spaces. They will need to know this information so they can make adjustments to their calculations and maybe put a sturdier structure in that area. You will need to coordinate between the structural engineer and the MEP engineer to identify any roof top units or other heavy items that need to be accounted for in the structure. You will also be coordinating the final grades from the civil engineer with the finish floor elevations from the structural engineer.

The MEP engineer will need to know special requirements for zoning, or if certain areas in the building have different HVAC requirements, such as a clean room with HEPA filter needs. They will want to discuss the ceiling height and clearances for their ducts, lights and plumbing lines so they can ensure all of it will fit. They will want to know the lighting plan for the rooms and the fixture type to include in order to provide the proper lighting levels and switching needs. You will discuss the power requirements, number of outlets and location of data/phone lines. The plumbing engineer will need to know the location of restrooms, sinks, or showers and will need to coordinate with the civil engineer to locate the wastewater locations.

Now would also be a good time to discuss critical items with any other consultants you might have on the team. Discuss the planting and irrigation strategy with the landscape architect and how it relates with the civil engineer's layout. Consider the different options for the roof with the roofing consultant and come up with ideas for the finishes with the interior designer. Speak with your accessibility specialist to identify any special considerations on the site or building that you need to look out for. In general, now is the time to get everyone started on the same page so they all know the expectations throughout the project.

Internally this is also the point that you will need to do some preliminary code analysis. You need to verify a lot of items that can dictate or change your preliminary design ideas and ensure you don't get too far into design before you realize you can do a five story building with no elevator, for example. Your first step in the code analysis is to identify all of the departments and codes you need to comply with. You will generally work from the overall project to specific components of the building, trying to ensure you have covered everything possible.

The first step is to look at the site as a whole and identify who the authority having jurisdiction (AHJ) is and what requirements they have. Find the city's planning document or visit the planning department and research the allowed uses on your specific site. Each lot in the city should have a specific use assigned to it and you need to make sure your building fits within that use. You can't put an industrial building in an area that is zoned for single family residences without a variance (that you are unlikely to get).

While you are at the planning level you need to see what kind of lot requirements the city has as well. They will indicate things as lot coverage area, or the amount of lot you are allowed to take up with the building, and setbacks, how far back your building needs to be from the front, back and side property lines. Most cities will also have requirements for building height, on-site parking requirements and landscaping standards. One critical component for you at this point is to also see if the city has any material or articulation standards that will dictate how the building will look and what material it will be made out of.

As you get past the site and start looking at the building you will start your building code research. The approved building code will depend on your jurisdiction and can vary from the International Building Code or International Residential Code and locally adopted codes. In general their purpose is the same, which is to give a guideline on how to design to keep the occupants safe. Your first step is to verify four key components that will dictate the form of the building; the allowable square footage, height, stories and construction type. These three all tie together and a change to one will change another, so it is about finding the best combination.

It works like this, the better the structure (more fire resistant), the bigger the building you can have, and the smaller the building, the less expensive type of structure will work. If you already know the square footage you need in the building, the code will tell you the minimum structure type you can have. If you have a small building, you could potentially build it out of standard wood framing that will cost less and possibly be faster and easier, but if you have a larger building, the structure might need to be made of a costly steel structure.

After you get beyond the overall building size and construction type you need to look further into the building and identify things like the occupancy classification and occupancy count. This is basically a designation of how the building will be used and thus how many people will be in the building at a given time. If a building is being used for business purposes it will have a lot less people in the building than a building that is being used for an assembly space. Each different type of use has different requirements for how many people will fit; whereas businesses with a lot of offices might only require 100 square feet per person, but assembly will be more crowded and could have only 5 square feet per person. As you get more people in a given space, the harder it will be to get them out in the event of an emergency.

Construction types:

Type V: Can be any type of construction. Is the least stringent on building materials, but is only allowed on smaller buildings. This will typically be used for stick framed wood construction.

Type IV: Also known as "heavy-timber", this construction is for really heavy duty framing; more than a typical stick framed building. We're talking 6" wood columns with 6x19 beams, etc. The idea on these is that a fire will not be able to burn through the thick wood quickly before smoldering, giving the occupants more time to exit.

Type III: Construction with noncombustible exterior walls, but combustible interior elements. This construction type is often used for masonry wall construction with standard interior partitions.

Type I and II: Noncombustible elements throughout, with the difference between the two being how many hours of fire resistance the elements have, with the more resistive falling into Type I. This construction type is typical of steel framed buildings.

Once you have your occupant load you will need to use this number to decide things like the number of exits you will need, how far apart they are spaced or how wide to make the corridors. You will also need to determine if the corridors or adjoining spaces will require a fire separation so a fire in one area will not jump over to the next space. This is based on differing levels of hazard, where the odds of a fire happening in say a garage, for example, are higher than in a residence. Thus, in this situation you need to try to separate the two from fire and smoke by building a fire rate wall between the two.

A lot of these calculations and research you have done so far will also be greatly affected by the addition of a fire sprinkler system, as it might allow you to add more square footage, building height, or modify your egress calculations. Fire sprinkler systems aren't cheap though, so make sure you consolidate your decision to add a sprinkler system with the owner's budget.

There are many other items that you will need to review in the code that are project specific such as multi-occupancy spaces, atriums, or mezzanines, that are all best approached as needed and reviewed by reading the code and reviewing with the architect. There are also many specific distance and calculations for egress out of the building that will need to be reviewed, but once you understand them they will become second nature for you as you design.

Things like the maximum travel distance to an exit, dead end corridors and separation of exits are all items you may not need to review every time as they don't really change, but you need to double check it anyways. The last half of most code books relate to very technical items that you won't spend a lot of your time reviewing, but at least know what they are and what they cover like structural, MEP and interiors.

BUILDING CODE ANALYSIS

APPLICABLE BUILDING CODE:	
APPLICABLE CODE YEAR:	
OCCUPANCY CLASSIFICATION: PRIMARY USE:	
OTHER USE(S):	
CONSTRUCTION TYPE:	
OCCUPANCY SEPARATION REQ'D:	
EXTERIOR WALL FIRE RESISTANCE:	
MAX ALLOWABLE FLOOR AREA:	
MAX BUILDING HEIGHT:	
MAX BUILDING STORIES:	
OCCUPANT LOAD:	

OCCUPANT TYPE	SQUARE FOOTAGE	SF PER OCCUPANT	OCCUPANT LOAD

NUMBER OF EXITS REQUIRED:	
MAXIMUM TRAVEL DISTANCE TO EXIT:	
COMMON PATH OF EGRESS TRAVEL:	
MINIMUM CORRIDOR WIDTH:	

10 Building Code Checklist. Downlaod at
http://www.architecturecareerguide.com/extras

You will also want to keep in mind the accessibility of the building and ensure you are following all the ADA rules as well. You want to make sure turning spaces in the rooms, clearances at the doors, accessible access between spaces and floor and correct heights for counters or controls. As you start laying out complex spaces like restrooms and break rooms, periodically verify that you are still complying with the accessibility rules so you are not discriminating against any users.

With the information you were able to coordinate with your consultants and the code research you conducted, you should have a better idea of how the building will actually start coming together. You then need to expand upon your schematic design documentation to incorporate all of these items. You might be adjusting your floor plan to accommodate a larger structural system, or you might be decreasing the height of the building to fit within the building code requirements. You might also start adding in the second floor construction with the required ceiling space required for the HVAC ducting. In this DD set you will also include more details on how the structure will interface with the rest of the building, details on how the ceiling lays in the space or basic door and window details. This is also the time to start listing out the finishes you expect in each room such as carpet, paint or wall coverings.

It is also at this point you need to start looking at products and materials that you will be specifying. As you design think about what you will be using in the space and start collecting cut sheets with product information that you will use later to produce the specs. These cut sheets could be for exterior finishes (siding, stucco, etc.), roofing materials, and plumbing fixtures, light fixtures or even paint colors. These can all be identified on the drawings or just kept in a binder to review as you go along.

The end product in the design documentation phase is a set of drawings that indicate a more refined building that has been vetted to meet the codes and has systems identified. It will include the architectural drawings as well as some preliminary civil, landscape, structural, MEP and interior drawings. It ties together all of the design decisions you made in the SD phase and how their scopes work within that. It will also include much more detailed design and starts to express how the design you had will be built, including details for the wall sections, enlarged plans or reflected ceiling plan.

DESIGN DEVELOPMENT
CHECKLIST

SITE
- [ ] ARCHITECTURAL SITE PLAN
- [ ] PARKING COUNT AND LOCATIONS (INCLUDING ADA)
- [ ] SITE FURNISHINGS
- [ ] EXTERIOR ELEMENTS (TRASH, GENERATORS, TANKS)

PLANS
- [ ] OVERALL FLOOR PLAN (1/8"=1'-0")
  - [ ] DOORS
  - [ ] WINDOWS
  - [ ] MILLWORK
  - [ ] OCCUPANCY SEPARATIONS
  - [ ] FURNITURE LAYOUT
  - [ ] STAIRS / ELEVATORS
- [ ] ROOF PLAN
- [ ] DEMOLITION PLAN
- [ ] FIRE / LIFE SAFETY PLAN
- [ ] REFLECTED CEILING PLAN
- [ ] ENLARGED PLANS
  - [ ] RESTROOMS, KITCHEN, MILLWORK

ELEVATIONS
- [ ] EXTERIOR ELEVATIONS
  - [ ] FIXED OR OPERABLE WINDOWS
  - [ ] DOORS
  - [ ] OVERALL DIMENSIONS
- [ ] EXTERIOR FINISHES / MATERIALS
- [ ] EXTERIOR LIGHTING LOCATIONS
- [ ] ROOF PROFILE AND MATERIALS
- [ ] INTERIOR ELEVATIONS

SECTIONS
- [ ] OVERALL BUILDING SECTIONS
- [ ] OVERALL DIMENSIONS

DETAILS
- [ ] EXTERIOR WALL DETAIL
- [ ] WALL TYPES
- [ ] DOOR & WINDOW SCHEDULES / DETAILS

PROJECT MANUAL
- [ ] INTERIOR FINISH / LIGHTING / SIGNAGE NARRATIVE
- [ ] SPECIALTY ITEMS NARRATIVE
- [ ] OUTLINE SPECIFICATIONS

11 Design Development Checklist. Download at
http://www.architecturecareerguide.com/extras

Construction Documents

Once you get into the Construction Documentation phase, the design should be pretty well defined. You should already know the type of building and its construction, its structural system and general locations of MEP systems. You will know where the building sits on the site and how it interacts with the surrounding landscape. It is at this point you need to take all the information you have in your head or in a general form on the drawings, and put it together into a package that somebody can build from. You will do this via the Project Manual that includes not only the drawings, but also the written specifications and project information.

The Drawings

The drawings are more than just a continuation of the design. They will go into more detail on the design, and should include every condition you feel needs to be properly documented in order to be built correctly. This includes items that maybe you haven't even seen in the previous drawings. You aren't just "zooming in" to the previous drawings, but virtually walking your way through the structure, building it with your mind. You need to look at your building as not just the final version but what are the steps that somebody needs to go through to get it to that final version. This is why it is so beneficial for interns to be given the opportunity to get out in the field and understand how buildings actually get built. Once you understand how it goes together you can get a better idea of what needs to be detailed.

Every project varies, but in general a lot of projects will follow this construction sequence, and as you go through each in your mind, think about what the contractor will need to know just for that phase, and make sure it is well documented in your drawings:

1. Lot clearing and grading. Before any work can begin on the building the site will need to be ready. This includes going through and clearing the site of any trees that are to be removed, underbrush cleaning and general site cleanup. Once there is a good, clean site to work with, the contractor will begin general site grading to make it match what the Civil Engineer dictated. Site grading consists of leveling the ground for the building to sit on, the parking areas and draining water away from the building.

2. Site utilities. The contractor will now start cutting trenches and laying down some of the required lines for electricity,

water, wastewater and possibly even irrigation. Make sure you coordinate with your Civil and MEP Engineers to verify all the necessary utilities are identified and located on the plans. Make sure you know where they are going into your building and what they tie into.

3. Building Pad/Foundation. The key to any good building lies in its foundation. It is critical to get this right before they even start building. The contractor will get the soil for the foundation set, as determined by the structural engineer or geotechnical engineer, by compacting the soil, removing the soil and bringing the right kind in, or treating the existing soil. They will begin laying out the form work for the concrete footings, grade beams, piers, or slabs. The rebar and building utilities that are integral will be placed in their proper spots and the concrete will be placed into the forms.

You will need to coordinate with the Structural Engineer to verify the foundation system being used and you will need to detail how your building will interact with this foundation. Detail how the wall will sit on the foundation and any anchor bolts needed. You should be aware of any underground conditions that will need to have special detailing for waterproofing. You also need to coordinate any in-slab MEP that needs to be located such as floor drains, toilets or vent lines.

4. Exterior Building Walls, Door/Window Frames. Once the foundation is set it is time to start going vertical. Depending on the type of construction this could be anything from wood framed walls, steel structure, CMU, or concrete walls. At this point they will also start putting in the door and window frames. You should start looking at every condition in relation to the walls. How it attaches at the bottom, sides and top. How it connects to other wall types, the roof or any soffits.

You need to look at every window for every condition from its sill, to the head and jamb conditions. You are detailing it for how it will sit upon the wall, how the wall is built around it and how you are going to waterproof it. This holds true for the doors as well. What are the thresholds going to be, are there double or triple studs at the jambs and is there a box header?

5. Roof. Now that the walls are up, they can begin building the roof to sit on it. They can either start framing it out, adding sheathing and waterproofing than the finish level, or pour concrete and add layers on top of that; it really

depends on the construction type. There are a few things to look out for here. You want to detail how the roof connects to the walls, if there are any overhangs, what type of pitch or slope the roof has, and what type of material is used. If there are any roof penetrations make sure you detail how those will be waterproofed and properly flashed as well.

6. <u>Interior Building Walls, Door/Window Frames, Ceilings.</u> Usually running concurrently with some of the exterior walls and roof, the framing for the interior walls take place. Interior walls differ from the exterior walls because they don't seal off the building envelope and are not always load bearing (but sometimes they are and should be coordinated with the structural engineer) These interior walls may have special conditions in how they are constructed for sound, fire, or even security purposes. Detail how these walls coincide with floor, exterior walls, roof and ceilings. Do these walls go all the way up to the roof, or do they extend only 6" above the ceiling? Do they have insulation in them, and if so, what kind? Locate and detail how the interior doors and windows are framed.

You need to also consider what kind of doors and windows are going in. Are they solid wood doors, hollow metal doors or aluminum? Are the windows single pane with tempered glass to protect from impact? You need to consider if there are any special devices or security features they will have, and importantly which doors will have locks, and what kind?

7. Interior MEP. Running concurrently with the interior walls, the contractor will begin installing the mechanical, electrical and plumbing systems. These will include the air conditioning and heaters, electrical outlets, toilets, sinks and drains. They will tie all of these lines into the site utilities that were laid out earlier by the Civil Engineer.

You need to decide and coordinate with an MEP engineer where all of the power outlets are, and what kind they are (duplex, quad or dedicated), and any switching requirements. You will start selecting light fixtures and laying them out in the space for not only aesthetics, but light levels and desired effect.

You will need to coordinate between the MEP, Architectural and/or Civil engineers where the units for the HVAC systems will go in the building or on the site. With the help of an MEP engineer, water heater system types will be determined and located and you will begin selecting plumbing fixtures. Make sure you detail and special conditions where the plumbing will sit in the millwork for accessibility purposes.

8. <u>Finishes.</u> At this point, the construction is getting pretty close to completed, but this is one of the most critical points in the final design, as you will need to detail the final finishes. Think of the room on each surface, and indicate what finish you want there. What is on the floor? Carpet, vinyl tile, ceramic tile or wood are all common selections and each needs to be detailed for how they will be attached to the floor and how you handle the transition between two different finishes. Think about how they work with the door swings or how they get finished at the walls. Do you want a floor base throughout the room, and if so, what profile?

Start thinking about each wall and the finishes they will receive. Paint, wall coverings, acoustic panels can be called out, but you also need to decide on the colors, the level of finish, how they will be attached and how they transition as well. Last is the type of ceiling in the room and its finishes. You can have painted ceilings, acoustic tile ceilings, floating clouds, or even exposed structures, and you need to detail how they interact with the walls, lights, HVAC or even the windows and doors.

Organizing your drawing set

Now that you understand the construction process, you have thought through every step of the way, and have considered the details, you need to organize everything on the drawings. A good starting point to put all of this info together is a "cartoon set". This is a mock-up set of drawings where you will create blank sheets and storyboard your set of drawings. You will determine what sheets are needed and start to decide what details will need to be generated. You can do this easily by printing out a number of sheets with your title block on it and just writing in the sheet name and details with a pencil as a place holder. By doing this you take all that you have thought about in the previous process and start putting together a set of drawings that will give the contractor everything they need to build the building.

The way we show the information needed for construction is through a series of two-dimensional drawings, each with their own unique needs. While currently technology is increasing to the level of being able to use three-dimensional building information modeling programs to build from, the majority of buildings still get built with pieces of paper, so it is still important to know how to put a set together. Plans, sections, elevations and details all have specific things they need to show.

The first thing people think of when imagining architectural drawings is a floor plan and this is for good reason as this is the main drawing that is usually the starting point to finding all of the other drawings. The floor plan is a two-dimension representation of cutting the building with a plane at 4'-0" and looking down.

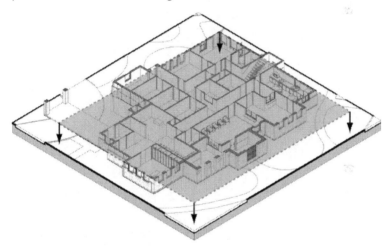

12 Isometric view of a floor plan

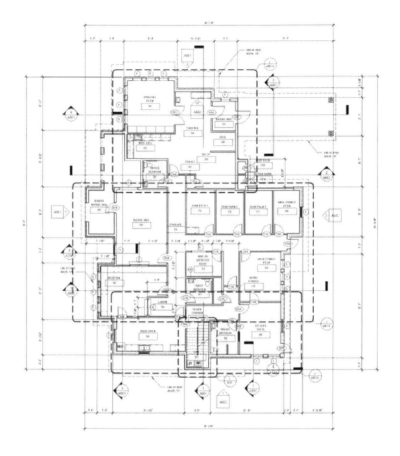

13 Two dimension floor plan

The floor plans show the location of walls, doors, windows, millwork, and anything that will be cut by the plane. There should be a string of dimensions throughout that show the location of all of these items and the overall dimensions as well. It is important to keep these dimensions clean and understandable without crossing over each other and not getting too cluttered. Floor plans will also contain a number of call outs for wall types, door and window numbering/types, and any special notes for items such as appliances. The drawing scale for most floor plans will be 1/8"=1'-0" or 1/4"=1'-0".

In addition to the overall floor plan, you will also create enlarged floor plans for specific items that need more detailing. Typical enlarged plans could be for restrooms, kitchens, locker rooms, entries or any room needing more detail. These plans will be zoomed in at a larger scale such as 1/2"=1'-0" or even up to 3"=1'-0".

Along with the floor plan and enlarged plans, another important drawing to have is the reflected ceiling plan. This plan will show what is going on at the ceiling. This plan is called such because it is drawn as if you cut the building with the same plane, and using a mirror, looked up at the ceiling, reflecting the plan. In this plan, it is important to show key features of the ceilings such as soffits or recesses and to show where things such as lighting and mechanical fixtures are placed.

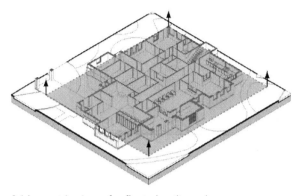

14 Isometric view of reflected ceiling plan

15 Two dimension reflected ceiling plan

Another major set of drawing that is used similar to floor plans are the exterior elevations. These drawings look at each vertical side of the building and will indicate heights, materials and general call outs for anything on the outside of the building. It is important to make sure the roof heights are coordinated to show the contractor where the tops of beams, floor plates or soffits are in relation to the ground level. You will need to call out what the materials are used on the outside of the building.

Looking further into the construction of the building you will detail building sections. Imagine taking a cutting plane to your elevation and looking in, and you will get an idea of a building section. Building sections are important to show the building structure, construction of floors and roofs and ceilings. They also show a relationship of the interior spaces to the exterior of the building, much like how floor plans show a square footage relationship, sections show a volumetric relationship.

Once we have a good feel for the floor plan, reflected ceiling plans, elevations and building sections, it is time to get into a little more detail on these drawings. You will need to start zooming in and showing how things are put together. Wall sections show how the wall is built, finished, waterproofed, and insulated. Door and window details show how these items interact with the walls and how they will be treated in the head, jamb and sill/threshold conditions. You will need to detail the floor, ceiling, roof and wall details with very specific instructions to the contractor.

CONSTRUCTION DOCUMENT CHECKLIST

SITE
- [ ] ARCHITECTURAL SITE PLAN
- [ ] PARKING COUNT AND LOCATIONS (INCLUDING ADA)
- [ ] SITE FURNISHINGS
- [ ] EXTERIOR ELEMENTS (TRASH, GENERATORS, TANKS)

PLANS
- [ ] OVERALL FLOOR PLAN (1/8"=1'-0")
  - [ ] DOORS
  - [ ] WINDOWS
  - [ ] MILLWORK
- [ ] ROOF PLAN
- [ ] DEMOLITION PLAN
- [ ] FIRE / LIFE SAFETY PLAN
- [ ] FINISH PLAN / SCHEDULE
- [ ] OCCUPANCY SEPARATIONS
- [ ] FURNITURE LAYOUT
- [ ] STAIRS / ELEVATORS
- [ ] REFLECTED CEILING PLAN
- [ ] ENLARGED PLANS
  - [ ] RESTROOMS, KITCHEN, MILLWORK

ELEVATIONS
- [ ] EXTERIOR ELEVATIONS
  - [ ] FIXED OR OPERABLE WINDOWS
  - [ ] DOORS
  - [ ] OVERALL DIMENSIONS
- [ ] EXTERIOR FINISHES / MATERIALS
- [ ] EXTERIOR LIGHTING LOCATIONS
- [ ] ROOF PROFILE AND MATERIALS
- [ ] INTERIOR ELEVATIONS

SECTIONS
- [ ] OVERALL BUILDING SECTIONS
- [ ] OVERALL DIMENSIONS
- [ ] EXTERIOR WALL SECTIONS

DETAILS
- [ ] EXTERIOR WALL DETAIL
- [ ] WALL TYPES
- [ ] ROOF DETAILS
- [ ] FLOOR DETAILS
- [ ] CEILING DETAILS
- [ ] DOOR & WINDOW SCHEDULES / DETAILS
- [ ] INTERIOR DETAILS
- [ ] ACCESSIBILITY DETAILS
- [ ] MILLWORK SECTIONS / DETAILS
- [ ] STAIR / RAMP / ELEVATOR DETAILS

PROJECT MANUAL
- [ ] SPECIFICATIONS

MISCELLANEOUS
- [ ] SHEET INDEX
- [ ] CODE ANALYSIS
- [ ] ENERGY COMPLIANCE / COMCHECK

16 Construction Document Checklist. Download at http://www.architecturecareerguide.com/extras

In construction, general contractors are responsible for the entire set of drawings, but will sometimes separate the drawings out to separate subcontractors with specialties.

The mechanical contractor may only see the MEP drawings, and the drywaller may only really look at the finishes sheet, so you need to keep this in mind when putting the drawings together.

One way to ensure it is clear is to keep it organized in a clear and understandable system. You want to keep any notes, callouts or details you have for finishes in one place, and don't sneak a note into a place that somebody wouldn't notice. Don't call out a specialized finish on a detail that shows mechanical equipment that only the mechanical sub will see. Another good habit to get into is to also only call something out in one place, which will help to eliminate confusion. If you have a floor plan and numerous details that call out to install carpet in a certain room, then at the last minute, you decide to change that to ceramic tile, you will have to go through and change everywhere it said carpet, and hope you get everyone, which doesn't always happen.

Specifications

In addition to the drawings we put together we also need to give the contractor specifics on what products we are using in the design, known as the specifications. The amount and way we call these specifications out will vary depending on the size of the project, but will typically consist of the product type/name, sizes, colors and installation methods.

For smaller projects, it may be possible to include the product information on the drawings themselves with notations and keynotes. On the elevation we could call out the type, color, size and/or how to install the materials. You can see that on small projects with few materials, this will be easy to find on one sheet, but for much larger projects, it could get cluttered fairly quickly. In those situations, we will put together "book specs".

In book specifications, each type of material falls within a specific category and is organized as such. Most architects, engineers and contractors currently follow a 50 division format as shown below with the most common listed:

Division 00 – Procurement and Contracting Requirements

Division 01 – General Requirements

Division 02 – Existing Conditions

Division 03 – Concrete

Division 04 – Masonry

Division 05 – Metals

Division 06 – Woods, Plastics and Composites

Division 07 – Thermal and Moisture Protection

Division 08 – Openings

Division 09 – Finishes

Division 10 – Specialties

Division 11 – Equipment

Division 12 – Furnishings

Division 13 – Special Construction

Division 14 – Conveying Equipment

Division 21 – Fire Suppression

Division 22 – Plumbing

Division 23 – Heating, Ventilation, and Air Conditioning (HVAC)

Division 25 – Integrated Automation

Division 26 – Electrical

Division 27 – Communications

Division 28 – Electronic Safety and Security

Division 31 – Earthwork

Division 32 – Exterior Improvements

Division 33 – Utilities

Every division is broken down to the specific material type further, such as 04 20 00 – Unit Masonry, with the first two numbers signifying the overall division and the next four giving more direction.

Within the specification there are three parts, 1-General, 2-Products, and 3-Execution. Part 1 will list a summary, related sections, submittal procedures and quality assurance. Part 2 will describe the products and any specific parameters necessary such as size and color. Part 3 will give specific information on how to install it such as pretreatment, tolerances and cleaning. By following the sequence of numbers, you might reference a direct specification section as 04 20 00 2.5 A 1 a.

Bidding and Negotiation

At some point in the project somebody will have to come on board and build the building, and this is a role typically filled by a contractor or construction manager. Once the contractor is on board the dynamic of the team (the owner and design team) changes as another party is now involved in the process. Many architects might view having to deal with the contractor a "necessary evil", but I think having a collaborative relationship with the contractor brings added benefits to the project.

The contractor is able to provide cost information based on their historical trends and current rates, and this is something we as architects just don't do every day, so why not leave that to somebody who has their finger on the pulse. Many contractors are also experienced enough that they have really good solutions to detailing some pretty complex conditions. There are many times that I have fallen back on the recommendation of a contractor because their solutions were more elegant.

While I feel that it is beneficial to have the contractor on board, not everybody shares this view. Unfortunately for some there is a history of an adversarial relationship between the contractor and architect. We both typically work for the owner and are not contractually tied to each other except for our contracts with the owner. This adversarial relationship and the tension it can potentially cause has led to many different delivery methods. A project can be built using a variety of methods including design-bid-build, construction manager and design build. Each of these delivery methods has their own merits and flaws and what is appropriate for one project might not be appropriate for others. Depending on the client, the method chosen might already be decided, or it can be decided as a result of recommendations by the architect. As you are selecting your projects to work on, keep in mind the clients preferred method or how you might fit into any one of these methods.

Design-Bid-Build

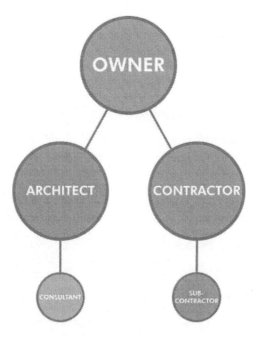

17 Design-Bid-Build or Traditional deliver method

This delivery method goes by many names, design-bid-build, traditional or competitive sealed proposal just to name a few. Any of those names make sense when you understand the process though. It is sometimes referred to as traditional method simply because it was the most common method used in the past, mostly because it was the only method. The way this works is the client hires you as the architect, and you work with the owner designing the building, and once the design is complete you put it out for general contractors to bid on how much they think it will cost. You will typically put this out to a few contractors in order to make sure you are getting a competitive price, and in order to be totally fair, they will submit the price at a specified time in a sealed envelope. This is done to make sure nobody knows ahead of time what the other contractors are charging and just undercut them to get the job. The hope is that you can get a good spread of numbers that are all accurate prices on how much it will cost, and not just "low bid" in order to get the project. Once a contractor is selected they get under contract with the owner to build it and you move into the construction contract administration phase. So in summary, this traditional method where you design it, they bid on the project (in a sealed proposal), which they eventually build upon. See how the "Design-Bid-Build" name fits in?

The benefit of this method is you get a number of general contractors competing against each other in an effort to present the best price, and in theory this will help get lower prices. If you have enough contractors bidding this can force them to really take a close look at how they can get a lower number, or "sharpen the pencil", so they have a better shot at getting selected by the owner. One thing that you have to look out for though is getting a contractor who submitted an inaccurate low bid in order to just get the job knowing they can charge the owner more for items later during construction. A mentor once told me, a lot of times the selected contractor is the one who "left the most out". Another concern with this method is that the accurate pricing doesn't come in until after the design is complete, and if the project ends up being over budget, the owner may ask the architect to modify the design or end the project all together.

This is the most common delivery method and has been the standard for many years for most owners. Many municipalities and private owners see the benefit of a competitive market, and with the help of a trusted architect, they can ensure they get a good contractor as well. This bodes well for us as the architect because it means we have some control over who we get to work with, but more importantly it sets us up in the role of being the professional assisting the owner, and establishes a lot of trust. With this delivery method however, you need to make sure everybody understands that you are here to work as a team to get the owner the best project possible and you don't want to set yourself up for a fight with the contractor because that will make the construction process unbearable.

If the owner decides they want to use this method you may be asked to put in a lot of work to help them out. Of course you will be doing the design as you typically do, but you also have to help with the creation of bidding documents, solicit for bids and issue addenda in order to assist the owner in selecting the contractor. At the end of the construction document phase you will begin the process of getting a contractor on board, but your work has to begin before you even get to this point.

In the project manual you will include a list of bidding information for the potential contractors. This will typically include the date that bids are due, the format they are to submit on and the process to ask questions. You have to spell out exactly how you want to see the bids so that everybody can be compared equally to each other.

Once the design is complete the owner will either invite a group of contractors to place a bid (invited or closed bidding), or place an ad for any interested parties to bid (open bid). For public projects they are typically required to only do open bids in order to allow for fair competition and the ad must run for a specified amount of time (usually 2 weeks minimum) and in local publications. For private projects, you can also just select one or more contractors to submit their prices, and many times the owner will ask for your recommendations on contractors you prefer to work with. You will also be involved in helping the owner schedule this as well since you have expertise in this area. If there is an advertisement it may run for a couple weeks and then you need to decide how long until you will expect the answers back. You need to take into consideration the size and complexity of the project as larger projects will take longer for all of the contractors to go through the drawings.

You also need to account for holidays, weekends, and working around specific days (like opening of hunting season here in Texas). You also need to decide how long it will take you and your consultants to answer questions that arise during the bid process and you have to spell out when questions are due and when you will get the responses back to them. This is an official process where you have to issue what are called addenda which either answer a question or provide a clarification and become an official part of the documents and must be issued to all potential bidders to be fair.

Before the bidding begins I also like to have a pre-bid meeting with all potential bidders. This is typical held at the site so they can get a feel for the project and will introduce everybody to the design team and owners. This is also the time to go over any special conditions of the project that need to be accounted for in the bid and to review the expectations of what the bids will include. It is also the time to discuss the schedule, to go through the drawings and specs if needed.

Once the bidding process starts the contractors are going to need to get their hands on some drawings to review, and how this is done can vary from project to project. The old way that is still used at times is to have the architect order extra copies of the printed drawings that they hold onto for potential bidders. The bidders can then put a deposit down to get a set of drawings, and if they decide they are not going to bid, return the drawings and get their deposit back. When the bidder is selected the extra sets of drawings can go to them for their use on the project or to the owner for their record. It is up to the owner or architect to keep a running list of bidders, often just referred to as the bidders list, and to make sure that all of the potential bidders are up to date with any changes. This is very time consuming for the architect and can be costly depending on how good you are at guessing on how many people will pick up drawings. The new method of doing this is to use a reprographics company that can print the drawings on demand and also can keep track of the bidders list as well. Most also offer to publish a pdf of your drawings on a special website that bidders can review before picking up the drawings.

Once the bidders have had a chance to review the drawings they will put together a package of their pricing and qualifications to the owner. This typically takes the form of a single sheet where they fill out how much money they will do the project for and sometimes the cost for alternately priced items. In addition to the price we will also ask for financial information to make sure they will not be going out of business soon (it happens), insurance information to make sure they are fully insured, a portfolio of previous similar projects, and resumes of the staff that will be a part of the project. When these packages come in, typically the owner and architect will both receive a copy for review and scoring. It is important for the architect to be a part of this process as this is something we deal with more often than the owner and they may need assistance in knowing what to review.

Once the bid packages are in and they have been reviewed, it is up to the owner to select the one builder they will execute a contract with. This selection can be nerve wracking for owners who are unfamiliar with the process, and that is where the architect steps in and helps with the scoring process. We can give our input on the contractor themselves, as it is not always just the price that is a factor. This can include the weighted scoring of such factors as quality of work, experience with previous projects and even who from the company will be working on the project. Obviously price is still an important factor, but it is critical to also consider these other items as they can make up for a lower quality builder who left a lot of money out of the bid to get the job.

The reality of Design-Bid-Build

I have had a lot of projects come in using this method and while the results have always been wonderful, two particular projects could not have been more different, and it always came down to my relationship with the contractor. At one end of the spectrum is a job that was a nightmare from day one and at the other is a job that might as well have been design-build because we really were a team.

In the first project mentioned we were hired to do a design for a non-profit client that I have worked for many times in the past. They decided that they wanted to bid this project out and see if they could get a good deal on their remodel work. We assisted them in the bidding process and even recommended a number of potential contractors. When the bids came in we scored the bidders and the owner selected the general contractor that had submitted the lowest bid, which ended up being 30% lower than the next lowest bid. We advised against it, but the owner decided to move forward anyways.

The contract was signed and we had our first meeting with the team and this contractor immediately started telling the owner that they couldn't build what we designed and how there were missing details. As the project progressed, issues came up that could not have been known beforehand due to this being an existing building, and the contractor would ask questions...a lot of questions, many unnecessary.

We would work through these and provide direction, but many times we would need to discuss the existing conditions as the contractor knew best what was actually in the field, but all we could ever get out of them is that they wouldn't move forward without a drawing from us first. At the end of the project everyone was unhappy and the owner ended up paying more than what was the highest bidder because of the change orders the contractor demanded. This contractor went out of business shortly after, but I don't know if I would have recommended them ever again anyways.

On the opposite end is a project where we designed a complex building for a repeat client and at the end of design it went out to bid. The budget for the project ended up being slashed and we went through a thorough value engineering process. Before we could finalize the value engineering phase the project was put on hold for a while for political reasons and didn't come back on until the next year. In the time it was put on hold it had to be re-bid and a new contractor was selected and started the construction of the project based on a list of verbal value engineering proposals from the owner. Due to the confusion on what was still in the project, some details were missed on the bids and some conditions had changed drastically. When these issues arose the contractor would call me and we would sit down and figure out a solution together, many times the answer coming from them. We were able to get through the project on budget and on time with the owner getting a better project than they could have hoped for, and all throughout the project it was a joy working with everyone. We still work together on many other projects that come up.

Construction Manager

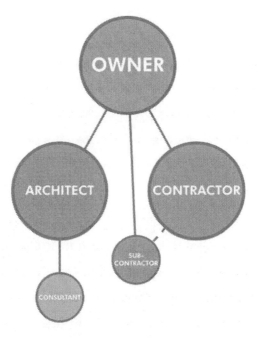

18 Construction Manager as Agent delivery method

The construction manager role is growing in popularity with many owners for a number of reasons and we are seeing a lot more projects being delivered this way. This method is very similar in that you have a person in charge of the construction of the building that is under contract to the owner and is not in a contractual relationship with the architect, but the main difference is they primarily act as a consultant to the owner. They typically do not perform the construction work themselves, but will manage all of the sub-contracting trades for the owner. There are two ways they can accomplish this, by being a construction manager at risk or a construction manager as agent. In a CM at risk method the subcontractors are all contracted directly with the CM and not the owner, meaning the CM assumes a portion of the risk on the project. The CM as agent method differs in that the subcontractors are contracted with only the owner, leaving the CM without any risk and serve in the role as a consultant to the owner only.

Regardless the role the CM plays (at risk or as agent), one of the major advantages is that they can be brought onto the project early and perform pre-construction services. These services can aid the owner and architect in making design decisions early on while taking costs and constructability into consideration. This is an important difference from the traditional method in that you are getting real time input from the person in charge of constructing the building and any changes you make can be done quickly and before getting too far along in the details. It also ensures that at the end of the design phase the owner is getting the best building for their money and it makes the construction contract administration phase go easier since the CM is already aware of a lot of items. The biggest drawback of this method is that you are stuck with just one CM and don't have a number of contractors bidding to have a lower price. The preconstruction services can also be an added expense to the project and can sometimes cost more than the owner could save with their recommendations.

For projects that are awarded via the construction manager role, the point at which the architect is involved depends on the owners comfort level with construction and their needs. Some owners want to have the construction manager on the team very early on to be able to give input on the design while others will wait until it is near completion before bringing them on. For the owners that are willing to pay extra for the additional pre-construction fees the CM will charge, they get the added benefit of having another team member that is an expert in estimating and constructability. This gives the owner the advantages of a design-build method, but without the concern of a conflict of interest on the part of the architect or contractor.

Doing this isn't cheap however, but if the owner is unsure of what they are doing, the extra money might be worth it. For owners that are a little more construction savvy, they might wait until the end of design development of 50% construction documents to have the CM give their input.

This gives them enough time to make design decisions that could have a major impact before it goes out to get all of subcontractors on board.

Regardless of when the CM is selected, most times the architect is brought on board first, and the owner will ask for assistance in selecting the CM. This could be as simple as giving your opinion, or can be as extensive as helping with contract negotiations. Most times the owner will handle the work of hiring the CM as they will be the one they are contracted with, but you might be asked to review their contract to make sure everything is included and there isn't anything missing. You could also be asked for your recommendations on CM's or to score the prospective bidders based on your opinion of their portfolio, price, previous experience with them, or other criteria applicable.

There are times as well that the owner may not want you to aid in the selection of the CM, but I would recommend you have some kind of involvement, as it shows your interest in helping the owner, while also making sure you have some control over who you will have to work with.

The reality of Construction Manager

The many projects I have been a part of that use the construction manager delivery method have generally been enjoyable and successful projects. In one project we brought on the CM at the end of design development and they were available for us to bounce design ideas off of and come to a great design. It was a very large project and while we had our thoughts on the best design, we had a lot of great ideas for improvement.

During the early design process we decided on a flat roof that used internal drains for aesthetic purposes and this is what we would have gone with if we didn't have a CM on board. The CM on this project recommended we consider switching it out to a single sloped roof with external drainage. We took this recommendation into consideration and began to look at what effect this would have on the design from an aesthetic and waterproofing perspective while they went out to their estimators and priced it out.

After reviewing their suggestions we liked the way it looked with a single slope and really liked the additional assurance of having fewer penetrations in the roof and potential issues with the internal drains. We were ready to give our recommendation that we move forward with their suggestions when they came back that this change would save us money. A win-win for everyone and this is the true value of the CM method.

Design Build

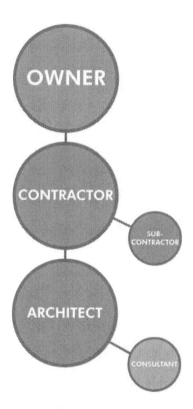

19 Contractor led Design-Build delivery method

This method is becoming more popular as owners, architects and contractors are looking to reduce the adversarial relationships and start and finish the project as a team. The way design build works is the person designing the building and the person constructing the building are already a team, or sometimes can even be the same person on small projects. When a team is put together for a design build project, they can take the form of contractor led or architect led. In a contractor led design build project, the contractor hires the architect to work under them and they answer directly to the contractor, while the architect led is the opposite. In the end the entire team is working directly for the owner and is ultimately responsible to them. The design build teams can be something that is all part of one firm and the architects and contractors all work for the same firm, or they can be assembled per project. Many architecture firms are becoming design build firms by performing the role of contractor themselves and this is a great way to ensure the project retains the integrity of the design.

The benefit of using a design build method is you get everybody working together all headed towards the same goal and you don't get bickering, posturing and politics you might get in other methods. You get the same benefit of early input on costs and constructability as the CM method as everybody is brought on early, and in fact it happens even sooner, so the design is that much tighter. The biggest flaw with this method is it loses the checks and balances that the owner gets in the other two methods of having two separate contracts. In the other delivery methods, each party (architect and contractor) is under separate contracts and their primary responsibility is to look after the owner. There is no chance of collusion happening where the architect design something that costs more just to get more money from the owner, or for the contractor to cut a corner just to save some money.

When you are already actively going after another job with somebody else, regardless of whether it is contractor or architect led, you are already building a relationship of trust with the contractor. You already know that you will back each other up if any issues arise and that you have each other's best interests in mind. The drawback to this is it is conceivable that while you are building trust with the contractor, you might be losing trust with the owner. You need to temper that potential perceived loss of accountability by ensuring the owner you have their best interest in mind first and foremost. The best way to do this is to be completely transparent.

When the project starts with a design-build method your fees as well as the contractor's fees will be tied into single pay applications under the same contract, so it is important to be able to let the owner know what they are paying for. You should have a separate line item for the design work than the construction items and it should be clear how this fee is broken down throughout the project. What you don't want to do is have it rolled into the overall price for the project and the owner is unsure what role you have in the process throughout. It is also important that the owner know that you are not running up the construction costs to get more for the contractor by involving them as much as possible in the decision making process. Provide options for them with the costs clearly defined so they can make the conscious decision and they understand why things are costing what they are.

Another way to display transparency is to be upfront with the owner when issues arise and don't try to cover them up by your relationship with the contractor. I once had a project that was delivered via a design-build method and an issue arrived during the construction that would have made the design-build team look bad in the eyes of the owner. We had neglected to coordinate a detail with the contractor and they could have easily covered it up and nobody would have known, but it was best to inform the owner that there was a mistake on our part that we were going to fix and already had a solution. By showing the owner that we made a mistake and admitted to it when it would have been easier to hope nobody noticed, we built trust with this owner and we continue to work with them to this day. In other delivery methods this issues could have become a major argument to whether the architect didn't design it right, or the contractor didn't build it right, with a lot of finger pointing, but in design-build everybody worked together to get it resolved.

If you find projects you are interested in doing via the design build method, there are a couple of ways you could go about this. For small projects that can be handled by smaller firms, you could just decide to start doing this yourself under architect led design-build. Start a firm that specializes in this construction type, get a contractor's license (if your state requires it), or hire a contractor to be a part of your firm. By selling yourself as a one-stop shop to potential clients you can find projects that are extremely helpful for clients who don't understand construction and just want to hire a team. For larger projects that might require a full construction team (estimator, project manager, supervisor, etc.), it might be best to get some working agreements with local contractors on a per-project basis. This could take the form of a verbal agreement to go after work together, splitting the costs for marketing with a contract at award of the project, or it can be a long term contract to provide services to each other. You could even go the route of forming a corporate entity for the group that is a separate company that is only in place for the life of the project.

Reality of Design-Build

Of all of the delivery methods I have been a part of, I have enjoyed my time doing design-build the most. Due to the project sizes I work on I haven't had the opportunity to lead a design build firm on a project, but I have been a part of contractor led design build teams in the past. I really enjoyed the team like atmosphere that is instantly created that last throughout the project and beyond. In one project we were selected along with a contractor, who we worked with many times in the past, as a design build team and we began the design process together. We attended weekly design meetings together and I would bounce ideas off of them and got immediate input on what effect that would have on cost and schedule. When we started out I had planned on using a pre-engineered metal building for a large portion of the building because of my assumption of their costs and speed, but when I discussed this with the contractor, they discussed that it would be cheaper to use their carpenters to build the same thing out of wood and would save them time in the phasing of the project. The design immediately went in that direction without having to wait for a revision to the drawings, a pricing exercise and subsequent approvals and change orders.

Be a professional

The bidding phase for each delivery method differs in that the owner will select and hire the contractor at different times and thus your role as the architect differs as well. Your role can vary from being a part of the team (design-build) to helping select the contractor (CM or traditional) and this is important in the relationship you will establish with the contractor. Whatever method is chosen, how they work out for you really relies on you and how you become a part of it. As the architect you are expected to be a professional advisor to the owner and regardless of how they contract with the person building it, you must still fill your role to the owner, as well as your most important role of protecting the health, safety, and welfare of the public. Embrace the team that will be put together and realize that regardless of who is contracted together, you are all after the same thing, creating a great building that is beneficial to everybody involved.

BIDDING AND CONSTRUCTION CHECKLIST

BIDDING

☐ SEND DRAWINGS TO PLAN HOLDER

☐ ORDER INTERNAL RECORD COPY

☐ BID ADVERTISEMENT

☐ PRE-BID MEETING

☐ ESTABLISH BIDDING SCHEDULE

☐ QUESTIONS & ADDENDA

☐ REVIEW / SCORE BIDS

CONSTRUCTION CONTRACT ADMINISTRATION

☐ PRECONSTRUCTION CONFERENCE

☐ ESTABLISH AND REVIEW PROCEDURES FOR DOCUMENTATION

☐ ESTABLISH CONSTRUCTION MEETING SCHEDULE

☐ DISCUSS REQUIREMENTS FOR PROJECT CLOSE OUT

☐ SCHEDULE 1 YEAR FOLLOW UP

20 Bidding and Construction Checklist. Download at
http://www.architecturecareerguide.com/extras

Construction Administration

As soon as the project is awarded to a builder and the owner has a contract with them the project enters what is called the construction contract administration, or typically shortened to construction administration or CA. This is when the construction begins and also where you find out if all that hard work during the documentation phase pays off. The architect is almost always involved in the CA role, but some architects feel that for smaller projects they are not needed during this phase. I personally don't agree with this, as I feel that I want to ensure the project turns out how I envisioned it. This is also the time when you can really connect with the owner and ensure future work.

Architects role in CA

This phase is technically called construction contract administration because the architect is not there to oversee the construction of the project, but rather ensuring that the builder is performing the work as required in the contract with the owner and the project manual. This includes observing the construction to verify that it is meeting the design intent for aesthetics and helping the owner validate the quality. The architect is not responsible for the construction of anything, the approval of anything or the observation of safety. These are all items that fall upon the contractor and the architect is only there to assist the owner with making sure they are getting what they are contracted for using our professional judgment. During this phase there is not a contract between the builder and the architect, only between the contractor and owner and architect and owner.

I have had the honor of dealing with a number of great contractors who have a great teamwork approach in mind, but at the same time, I have had some poor ones as well. There is a history of architects and contractors not getting along for various reasons, maybe the contractor thinks the architect is egotistical with unnecessary perfectionism, while the architect thinks the contractor is only trying to cut corners. Whatever the reasons might be, it's never good for anybody on the team, and especially not for the owner, and in the end that is who we all work for, so we should make sure they are happy.

I once had a contractor that I was working with insist that he knew better than me because he had been working as a contractor longer than I was alive and because of this he went out and built something completely different than what was shown in the detail I put together, feeling he knew better. This went unnoticed for a while until the building inspector showed up and questioned him about it. It turns out the codes had changed a bit and what he built no longer met the requirements. He had to tear it out and rebuild it at cost to his profit and ego.

I also have had many times when an issue came up in the field that I needed to address immediately, and after literally hours of coming up with different schemes and details, none of which were working, the contractor came up and said, "I see what you are trying to do, but why don't you just do it like this." He proceeded to literally draw his idea in the dirt and it was like getting hit with a ton of bricks, "Why didn't I think of that!"

As you can see, contractors and architects both bring different skills to the team and it is only in the manner of teamwork that we can produce the best building possible. Remember, in the end, the goal is to provide the owner with the best building possible, and we, the contractor and architect, should always be working towards that.

Meetings

As much as we hate to admit it, we need to have meetings during the CA phase to ensure a smooth project. While we can limit the time we spend in the meetings, they can be some of the most productive times in the project because everyone is in the same room and communicating. Communication is key to a successful construction project, and if you want to have an environment where everyone is part of the team, you must have meetings.

When the project first gets started, this is the best time to have a meeting and set the ground rules for how the project is going to go. This is typically referred to as a "kick-off meeting" and involves the owner, architect, contractor, special sub-contractors and required design consultants. This is separate from the kick-off meeting that the contractor may have with their own sub-contractors, but serves the same purpose, to set some ground rules. I like to initiate this meeting as it shows the owner that you are proactive and that you are doing all you can to protect their interests. As an intern, you might not get a chance to attend these meetings, but if you do it is critical to pay attention to who all of the players are and how they relate to each other. In these meetings I will introduce all of the team members and go through the project information based on the project manual. We will discuss things like methods of communication, points of contact, who is responsible for what and what the expectations of the owner are. It is good to make sure everybody understands who and how they discuss things that come up during the construction so that nothing slips through. We will also discuss things that the owner might have a requirement for like hours of construction, where the contractor needs to park, and who is paying for the utilities until the owner moves in. While these might seem like boring administrative discussions, it is necessary to make sure everyone is on the same page before problems arise.

At the kick-off meeting I will also discuss what the plans are for meeting during the construction process. Depending on the size and scope of the project, it is good to have periodical meetings with the architect, contractor and owner to discuss any issues that may arise during construction. These can be anywhere from weekly meetings to monthly meetings depending on the complexity and coordination necessary. These meetings are a good chance for interns to attend as there are a lot of them, but you typically won't be expected to go alone and answer questions. What we typically talk about during these meetings is any outstanding questions the contractor has, and new questions they have, how the project is progressing and any budget issues that may come up. At the conclusion of the updates, we also have the option to walk around the site and observe the general construction. If you are asked to attend a construction meeting, be sure to take all safety measures required (closed toe shoes, hard hat, safety vest) and pay attention. There will be construction going on and some of those not-as-good sub-contractors might like to mess with you (it happens).

I remember as a young intern going to my first job site and you could tell I was nervous. I pulled up to the site and had on my new, shiny hard hat and vest with not a scratch to be seen. I checked in at the jobsite trailer and went on my way to document and photograph a field condition my boss had asked for. On the way there I had to go through a gauntlet of iron workers who all seemed to stop what they were doing to watch me. I knew not to look directly at the welding, I steered clear of their ladders and generally minded my own business. Suddenly out of nowhere there was a loud "bang" just a few feet from me and it made me jump a bit on the inside. As I looked over I realized that there was a worker there banging on a piece of steel with a huge hammer looking me dead in the eye. There was no reason for him to be hitting the steel as they weren't even working in the area, but I guess razing the punk kid is reason enough. I kept my calm and went on to my task and didn't let it bother me. After numerous more visits like that, I gained more confidence and everybody seemed to realize that it didn't faze me, so they left me alone after that. It is important to remember that you have every right to be there just like them, and so long as you are being safe you should be of no consequence to them.

In addition to the construction site meetings and field visits, there are times when you might be asked to attend special meetings with the owner. These can be to discuss items the owner is installing themselves such as furniture, audio/visual or appliances, or can be to discuss things like colors/finishes. There are times when it is beneficial for the owner to buy and install items themselves and they need to coordinate this with the overall construction process. You might need to locate where these are to go, or just make sure they will work for what the owner wants. It is also beneficial to take a look at colors in a space once it is mostly built out. You might meet with an interior designer and hold up paint chips and finishes to see what it will look like in the space itself.

Any time you visit the job site, you should also put together what is called a field report. It is a document that shows the conditions as we see them and any items we need to bring to the owners attention. Depending on the project, the owner may not always be able to make it out to the site, and besides, they may not see the same thing we do. We typically log information such as weather, participants and time, but more importantly we log any conversations we have with the contractor and any issues that are noticed. These field reports are official documents, but are also communication tools to make sure everybody is on the same page.

As an intern still learning your way around the practice of architecture, I feel that attending meetings can be a great education, but you have to be an active listener. Many things you may not understand, in fact I would say most things you won't understand, but it is important to still listen to what is going on. Write down any words or acronyms you don't understand and ask your supervisor about them later, or search them on the Internet. The more you are a part of these meetings you will start to find that you are really getting it, and eventually you will be able to offer ideas and solutions. You might pick up some bit of information you store for later and then you hear it discussed in a later meeting solidifying what you understood. These bits of information keep building up until you are comfortable with any issue that comes up.

Documentation

Once construction begins there is a process we must go through to make sure the owner is getting what they want, and making sure the contractor is on the same page as us. This can generally take the form of submittals, schedule of values and applications for payment, but can also include overall schedule and punch lists.

As part of the specifications, we typically ask the contractor to provide us with documentation of what they plan on furnishing and installing on the project so we can review them for the owner. We would typically see some form of documentation for every item we specify, from the metal studs to the window blinds. Our role in this is to review the documents and either take no exception to them, make notes on them or reject them. As we are not in a contractual relationship with the contractor, we also do not approve the items. This is a fine line, and really comes down to liability, but we cannot be expected to catch every little detail in the submittal, so we are not guaranteeing that what the contractor wants to use will meet all the requirements. It is up to the contractor to also check the drawings before they get to the architect. Submittals can take the form of product data, shop drawings or samples.

When reviewing product data, we typically check them to make sure they meet the requirements for the project, as well as any third party requirements such as NFPA or ICC. These are third party testing methods that describe how the product should conform, and we want to make sure they meet these testing methods. We also want to check to make sure meet project specific requirements such as sustainability (recycled content, VOC limits) or for compatibility with other products. If the contractor would like to substitute a product for one that we specified, this is also the time that we will review it.

Shop drawings are generated by the sub-contractor building a specific component, such as cabinetry, and we check these for dimensional accuracy and construction methods. We will review these in comparison with the contract documents, with product data and other components. In the example of cabinetry, we will check that the cabinets are the right size, built the right way and with the right material, but we will also check them against the cabinet hardware product data to make sure they will all work together.

Samples are generally smaller versions of the actual product that will be installed. This can be for items such as paint, wall coverings, aluminum windows, or ceiling panels. We check these samples with the samples we used in the design, or with other samples of neighboring materials. There are times when a finish or color isn't selected, and the contractor will provide a set of samples for the architect to choose from. It is important during this time that we also receive all finish samples together so we can judge them next to each other and not separately.

In addition to the paper submittals, many projects also include the requirement for a sample mockup. Much like a finish sample, this sample is a smaller version of the actual building. It can vary in size from a 4' panel to a 10'x10' corner condition. The intention of this mockup is to show how the contractor plans on building every condition, from concrete to siding to windows. Once the architect and owner review the mockup for construction details and finishes, the contractor will then use the mockup as a sample of what is expected throughout the building. This mockup can also be a part of the actual finished building if allowed by the owner/architect. This is also a good opportunity to test the construction for water penetration. With a window in the mockup you can take a garden hose and spray it down, or have a third party testing company test it to see if it leaks.

As tedious and monotonous as checking submittals and shop drawings are, many supervisors will ask interns to do the initial reviews for them. This can seem like a punishment, but if you look at it the right way, this can be a great opportunity for you. By reviewing the shop drawings you are getting information directly from the expert on how they would build something and it only serves to reinforce the details you were pulling together for your boss. It also forces you to look at the building as a series of intricately designed details that combine to create the whole. When you're in school you look at the form and massing and general aesthetics, but in the real world, it is the little details that make the difference in good and great architecture, and you are getting a chance to be a part of every little piece of the building.

Payments

In our role of assisting the owner during the construction process, we are also responsible to sign off on pay application, or pay apps for short. The purpose of this is to help the owner, using our professional judgment to make sure the contractor is billing for work that was actually completed. At the beginning of the project, the contractor will typically submit a schedule of values that will list out every single type of item they will install or task they will perform during the project. There will be fees associated with these items so that the owner can get a good feel for how the costs break down. Depending on the project, we can also ask that the schedule of values (SOV) be broken down by labor and materials, so we can verify the costs of items as well.

Each month the contractor will submit an application for payment to the owner. The architect will review it to see the progress the contractor is claiming to have made and sign off for the owner to pay, or review inconsistencies with. In a typical pay application, the contractor can bill for work performed, items purchased and installed, or items purchased and stored. We typically would want to make sure that these items that are stored be in a bonded or secured facility. If the owner is going to pay for the items, we want to make sure they don't lose out if somebody breaks in and steals them. Each month when the owner pays the contractor, there will also typically be a retainage that is held out of the payment. This is a certain amount of money, usually a percentage of the bill that is set aside until the end of the project. The purpose of this is to ensure that the contractor finishes the job and doesn't just walk away before the end.

It is also important on some projects to check the payment applications for a release of liability from the sub-contractor to the owner. On any project, it is generally the requirement of the general contractor to pay their subcontractors, but in the event that this doesn't happen, the subcontractor can place a lien on the owner's property until they are paid. This is to defend the subcontractors from not getting paid and gives them a way to get their money. Once their portion of the work is complete, we want to make sure for the owner, via a lien release, that the general contractor has paid their subcontractors and they will not be placing a lien on the owner's property.

Many times the review of the pay application will not be an intern's responsibility, but you should still know how to read one. If the contractor is using a standard AIA form, the information will always look the same. The front page is usually a summary and the first thing you want to check is that the contractor has done their math right. Double check their calculations to make sure they are asking for the right amount and that all of the numbers match. On the subsequent pages is their breakdown of the project and this should match the schedule of values they sent you at the beginning of the project. Go through each item and verify the amount they say they have already completed and billed, the amount billed this month and the remaining. You want to make sure that the percentage of work they are claiming to have completed this month matches what is estimated out in the field. Check the totals and double check that they are taking out the retainage. Depending on the project, you might also get the "backup" for this month's bill, which usually consists of the invoices from their subcontractors for the work they performed and any other releases or notarized documents.

Design Opportunities

Throughout the construction process there will inevitably be some changes to the design. Whether it is a detail not thought of before, or something that was not caught, it all needs to be documented properly. Something to remember is that there really no such thing as a perfect set of drawings. We as architects have to visualize an entire building in our minds, with the help of tools, but it is impossible to think of every single condition that will arise. You strive to have as much detail as possible, but there will always be something that is missed. What is important is not trying to have a perfect set of drawings, but being able to react to the issues when they arise. There are a number of ways we can deal with problems (or as my former boss called them "design opportunities") and how we document them depends on how they are noticed.

If the contractor is unsure of the design of something, whether it is a specific detail, or product, they will issue a request for information, or RFI. The RFI will document the issue in question, and can also include a proposed solution, which is then forwarded to the architect to answer. The architect will answer the question or forward to one of the consultants to answer, and send a response within a certain amount of time. Sometimes the response will be in the form of a written answer, or can include an additional sketch.

For issues that are noticed by the architect or owner, the appropriate documentation will take the form of an architect's supplemental instruction, or ASI. The ASI is a documented change to the contract documents that will not affect cost or schedule, and is considered an addition the drawings. This could be a detail that wasn't put into the original sheets or just a clarification, but they should not be for additional work or products not already in the cost or schedule.

Proposal requests are similar to ASI's, except they will affect costs or schedule, as they might be for additional work or a change in products. A proposal request will be put together by the architect and forwarded to the contractor for response. The contractor can respond with a change order that will incorporate any changes in cost or schedule for the owner's approval. If the owner is comfortable with the changes, they will sign the change order and they will become a part of the contract documents. If the owner does not approve of the change order, there is no change to the original contract documents.

Besides being a part of the construction meetings and shop drawings, I feel one of the best educations you could get is by going through the RFI's and ASI's. When a contractor sends in an RFI, you get an idea of the issues that come up during construction that you can make note of and make sure is clear on the next project. You get to see how the architect responds and how the relationship works between the two and how everybody has to work together during construction. I said earlier that there is no such thing as a perfect set of drawings, but I feel that if the production staff putting together the drawings knew every single question the contractors had, it would increase the quality of the next set of drawings exponentially.

Project Closeout

At the end of the construction process, the architect's role is not done. This is when it is most critical that the architect be present to ensure that the final product is exactly what the owner wants, immediately afterwards and many years after. Our role is to make sure the owner gets a quality, finished building as well as making sure any warranties are in place and the contractor is paid their retainage.

When the contractor thinks they are substantially complete, they will submit a list of items they know still needs to be completed, also known as a punch list, before final completion. While it is supposed to be the responsibility of the contractor to provide the punch list for the architect to verify, most of the times it falls on the architect to create their own punch list. Our job is to check to see if we believe they are substantially complete with just some minor items left to finish. What usually ends up happening is that there are still a lot of things left to fix that we notice, so it's better off if we just create our own punch list.

In the review of the project for substantial completion we will typically walk through every space of the building and look at every square inch of the building. We are looking for any flaws in construction or defects in products that we feel need to be replaced before the contractor leaves. We will check for things such as final paint finishes, carpet seams, ceiling tile alignment and that final cleaning has taken place. I have had some contractors tell me they have a "zero punch", meaning there are no items that are not complete, but that just sounds like their standards of care are low. Just as there are no perfect drawings, there are also no perfect buildings. There are also some architects who take pride in creating multiple pages worth of items that they noticed need to be fixed, but many of the items are extremely minor, but this just breeds contempt. In the end, the purpose is to give the owner a building we are all proud of.

If we feel that the project is not substantially complete, we will not sign off on it. This is critical, because this date of substantial completion is what triggers many items such as warranties and certificates of occupancy. Most contractors will have a one-year warranty on the work they performed in addition to the warranties on the products, and that one-year doesn't begin until the date of substantial completion. So if anything happens in the building that the contractor needs to fix within a year, they must come back and fix it, so it is in the best interest of the owner to make sure that one-year period doesn't start early. The city will also not allow the owner to move into the space until it is substantially complete, so the owner can't start using the space until we sign off.

During this project closeout period we will also start collecting documents for the owner. We typically need as-built drawings from the contractor that notes any changes to the drawings in the actual building for record purposes. We also request any operations and maintenance (O&M) manuals and copies of all warranties. It is also a good idea to schedule training with the owner and any users to make sure they know how to use and maintain their new building.

Once we have signed off on substantial completion, all of the closeout documents are in and the final punch list items are fixed we make one last trip to make sure there are no remaining items left to fix. If everything is completed, we will sign off on the final pay application that will pay the contractor out for the remaining amount left on the contract as well as any retainage we held back. Now all is left to do is celebrate another successful project.

Interns in CA

As an intern some of the best education you can get to become an architect is to be a part of the construction process. It is the most beneficial phase at an early phase, but it can also be the most stressful. It can be nerve wracking to go out there on the job site and be surrounded by a bunch of seasoned professionals using a secret language, but the fastest way to learn anything is to be immersed in it. Surround yourself with people on a higher level and learn from them and you will get there eventually. Be professional, be confident and be an active listener and you will be asked back to more meetings and do visit the site more often, meaning you will be learning faster.

BIDDING AND CONSTRUCTION CHECKLIST

- -

BIDDING

☐ SEND DRAWINGS TO PLAN HOLDER

☐ ORDER INTERNAL RECORD COPY

☐ BID ADVERTISEMENT

☐ PRE-BID MEETING

☐ ESTABLISH BIDDING SCHEDULE

☐ QUESTIONS & ADDENDA

☐ REVIEW / SCORE BIDS

CONSTRUCTION CONTRACT ADMINISTRATION

☐ PRECONSTRUCTION CONFERENCE

☐ ESTABLISH AND REVIEW PROCEDURES FOR DOCUMENTATION

☐ ESTABLISH CONSTRUCTION MEETING SCHEDULE

☐ DISCUSS REQUIREMENTS FOR PROJECT CLOSE OUT

☐ SCHEDULE 1 YEAR FOLLOW UP

21 Bidding and Construction Checklist. Download at
http://www.architecturecareerguide.com/extras

Conclusion

Now that you have made it through the guide, you should now feel more confident in knowing the basics of what happens in an architecture practice. You have learned how to get your first job and how architecture should be treated as a business. You can take the knowledge you have on how architecture firms find work and get out there to find some clients of your own. Once the client is there, you can now put together a good design and drawing set that the contractor can build from, and you will be fully involved in the construction process.

By learning these things you will be years ahead of most architects who are still learning these things. You will still have to put all of the knowledge into practice in order to truly learn, but it all starts with the knowledge. Take what you have learned and apply it. Ask your supervisor for more responsibility and impress them with your confidence.

This will get you started in your architecture career, but that is not all there is to architecture. There are nuances to running the business, marketing, extra services, specializing and niche markets, all of which go above and beyond just design. This book is just the start of what you need to know, by giving you a great foundation to build from. So once you have the basics down, keep learning and growing.

I hope you found this information helpful and that it will answer all of the questions you have, but if you have more questions, go to http://www.architecturecareerguide.com and send me a message or leave a comment.

Also, go to http://www.architecturecareerguide.com/extras to download all of the bonus material.

Appendix A: Common Abbreviations

AB : Anchor Bolt

ABV : Above

AC : Air Conditioning

ACT : Acoustic Ceiling Tile (see Lay-in)

ADA : Americans with Disabilities Act

ADJ : Adjacent

AFF : Above Finished Floor

AHJ : Authority Having Jurisdiction

ALT : Alternate

BM : Beam

BTM : Bottom

BTW : Between

BUR : Built Up Roof

CFCI : Contractor Furnished, Contractor Installed

CIP : Cast In Place (Concrete)

CJ : Control Joint

CL : Center Line

CLR : Clear

CMU: Concrete Masonry Unit

CONC: Concrete

CPT : Carpet

CT : Ceramic Tile

DIA : Diameter

DIM : Dimension

DN : Down

DR : Door

DS : Downspout

DW : Dishwasher

EA : Each

EF : Exhaust Fan

EJ : Expansion Joint

EL : Elevation

ELEC: Electrical

ELEV : Elevation or Elevator

EQ : Equal

EWC : Electric Water Cooler

EXH : Exhaust

EXIST : Existing

EXT : Exterior

FD : Floor Drain

FDC : Fire Department Connection

FE : Finished Edge or Fire Extinguisher

FEC : Fire Extinguisher Cabinet

FF&E : Furniture, Fixtures and Equipment

FIXT : Fixture

FLR : Floor

GA : Gauge

GFCI : Ground Fault Circuit Interrupted

GLB : Glue Laminated Beam

GWB : Gypsum Wall Board (see Drywall, Gyp. Bd)

GYP : Gypsum

GYP. BD. : Gypsum Board

HB : Hose Bib

HD : Head

HDR : Header

HM : Hollow Metal

HVAC : Heating, Ventilation and Air Conditioning

ILO : In Lieu Of

INSUL : Insulated

INT : Interior

KD : Knock Down

LAM : Laminate

LAV : Lavatory

LH : Left Hand

LHR : Left Hand Reverse

LKR : Locker

LVL : Laminated Veneer Lumber

MDF : Medium Density Fiberboard

MECH : Mechanical

MIN : Minimum

MR : Moisture Resistant

MTL : Metal

NIC : Not In Contract

NOM : Nominal

NTS : Not to Scale

O/ : Over

OA : Overall

OC : On Center

OFCI : Owner Furnished, Contractor Installed

OH : Opposite Hand or Overhead

PL : Plastic Laminate

P.LAM : Plastic Laminate

PT : Pressure Treated

RCP : Reflected Ceiling Plan

RD : Roof Drain

REF : Refrigerator

REQ'D : Required

REV : Revision

RH : Right Hand

RHR : Right Hand Reverse

RO: Rough Opening

ROW : Right of Way

S4S : Surfaced Four Sides

S&S : Stained and Sealed

SC : Solid Core

SIM : Similar

SPEC : Specification

SQ : Square

SS : Stainless Steel

STC : Sound Transmission Coefficient

STD : Standard

STL : Steel

STRUC : Structural

T&B : Top and Bottom

T&G : Tongue and Groove

TO : Top Of

TOC : Top of Concrete or Top of Curb

TOS : Top of Steel

TOW : Top of Wall

TS : Tube Steel

TYP : Typical

UNO : Unless Noted Otherwise

VCT : Vinyl Composition Tile

VIF : Verify in Field

W/ : With

W/D : Washer and Dryer

W/O : Without

WB : Wind Brace

WC : Water Closet

WD : Wood

WIC : Walk In Closet

WF : Wide Flange

WH : Water Heater

WWF : Welded Wire Fabric

Made in the USA
Columbia, SC
06 May 2019